BUILDING A CAREER

The Effect of Initial Job Experiences and Related Work Attitudes on Later Employment

Joseph A. Raelin
Boston College

THE W.E. UPJOHN INSTITUTE FOR EMPLOYMENT RESEARCH

Library of Congress Cataloging in Publication Data

Raelin, Joseph A 1948-
Building a career.

Bibliography: p.
1. Young adults—Employment—United States—Attitudes—Longitudinal studies. 2. Job satisfaction—United States—Longitudinal studies. 3. Job satisfaction literature—United States. I. Title.
HD6273.R33 331.3'4 80-24848
ISBN 0-911558-74-8
ISBN 0-911558-73-X (pbk.)

300 South Westnedge Ave.
Kalamazoo, Michigan 49007

THE INSTITUTE, a nonprofit research organization, was established on July 1, 1945. It is an activity of the W. E. Upjohn Unemployment Trustee Corporation, which was formed in 1932 to administer a fund set aside by the late Dr. W. E. Upjohn for the purpose of carrying on "research into the causes and effects of unemployment and measures for the alleviation of unemployment."

The Author

Joseph A. Raelin is director of the Institute for Public Service at Boston College. He is also assistant professor of management. Raelin received the Ed.M. in counseling from Tufts University, the C.A.G.S. in organizational development from Boston University, and the Ph.D. in policy studies from SUNY at Buffalo where he was a Ford Foundation fellow. He continues to serve as a management consultant to many firms and agencies in the Boston area, as well as to the Department of Labor on a major national legislative redesign.

Dr. Raelin's teaching and research interests are in public policy and human resources management, particularly at the macro level. His publications in the quality of worklife area include, in addition to the present volume, his applied research in public service employment programs and in part-time work alternatives.

Dedicated to
Jonathan,

in hopes that his first job and later experiences will be as bright as he.

Acknowledgements

The author wishes to acknowledge the support of this research by the W.E. Upjohn Institute for Employment Research, under Research Grant Agreement No. 78-04-13. Dr. E. Earl Wright, Director of the Upjohn Institute, provided many helpful comments and was consistently supportive for the duration of the research grant. Although acknowledging the support of the Upjohn Institute, the author naturally assumes full responsibility for the contents.

The author also wishes to extend his appreciation to Boston College, in particular to Dean John J. Neuhauser of the School of Management, for providing the necessary environment for conducting this kind of research. The University's Offices of Research Administration and Contracts and Grants, and especially John O'Toole, are also to be commended for their grass-roots support at all stages of the project.

Appreciation is extended to research assistants Lois Greenfield, Joseph Gannon, and Ann Stravalle, for their deft handling of the many phases of this project, from codebook preparation to literature reviews; and to John Havens for his expert consultation during the formative stages of the project. Carol Davis did the finishing touches on all the artwork and provided many helpful suggestions on the figures. The entire manuscript except for chapter 2 represents the typographical work of Mrs. Mary McCourt, secretary to the Institute for Public Service, and reflects her high caliber of professional work. Chapter 2 was adeptly prepared by Lisa Schmidt. Finally, moral support for the entire project was provided gratuitously by the author's patient wife, Abby Raelin.

Foreword

Public policy on youth employment has focused primarily on job creation programs designed to meet the problem of continuing high levels of youth unemployment. Policymakers have had little information, however, on the long term effects of work experiences acquired through such programs as public service employment. Dr. Raelin's findings suggest that the qualitative aspects of initial job experience are likely to be critical in shaping later work attitudes, aspirations, and ultimate employment.

Raelin has developed a causal model of early career development to examine the relationship between different occupational characteristics and job satisfaction and the relationship of the job satisfaction measure to general work attitudes. He concludes with specific recommendations of relevance to present youth employment policy.

Facts and observations presented in this monograph are the sole responsibility of the author. His viewpoints do not necessarily represent positions of the W. E. Upjohn Institute for Employment Research.

E. Earl Wright
Director

Contents

List of Illustrations

Table

Figure

Chapter 1
Introduction

Policy Problem

There are about 15 million American youth, between the ages of 16 and 24, no longer in school, who are employed in the labor force at the present time. Many of these youth are new entrants into the labor force, therein having an initial job experience. Some of these youth have been with their first job for awhile. Upwards of a million youth are also getting an initial job experience through government employment programs which provide a variety of work and training experiences, particularly for the disadvantaged. This latter number does not include the over one million short term jobs provided each year by the nation's Summer Youth Employment Program.

It has been this author's observation that the focus of public policy with respect to the alleviation of the problems of unemployment in this country from a countercyclical jobs perspective (apart from fiscal and monetary tools), whether it be for youth or the general population, has been on *speed* and *quantity*. In other words, and this can be demonstrated by reviewing any of the histories of federal manpower legislation, where money has been appropriated the message to employment and training administrators has been: "Get as many jobs as you can fast!" This focus, although resolving a short term employment problem, may not have addressed, except perhaps adversely, the long term employability problem of youth. Indeed, whether initial youth employment experiences are organized through direct public policy vehicles or through the interplay of market forces in the private or public labor markets, human resource managers and policymakers have little information to ascertain the long term effects of such job experiences on the youth population as a whole or its subpopulations. Specifically, policymakers need to know more about whether the qualitative aspects of initial job opportunities, including their contribution to early and mid-term job satisfaction, have any effect on later work experience. They also need to know whether other career attitudes, such as aspirations or motivation, separately or in combination with the job, affect later work experience. Furthermore, can mid-term job changes disrupt successful or aggravate unsuccessful career paths? How rigid are initial job attitudes; do they become generalized or can subsequent work experience readily change them? Such concerns as these need to be addressed especially with regard to young people entering the labor force, since their initial experiences are likely to be most critical in shaping their future work dispositions and practices.

Core Model

The premise of this study is that in the early career of a young person's life, initial job experiences and attitudes are critical in shaping ultimate employment experience. The study is longitudinal in character, such that essentially snapshots are taken of a youth sample at three different times in their early careers. The interval separating the early and late periods, corresponding to data end-points, is nearly ten years. The mid-point is around the fifth year. The study's design is a path model, referred to here as the "core model," which hypothesizes a set of multiple, recursive relationships among a set of time-specific, work-related variables which have been selected because of their expected contribution to a theory of initial job experiences and later employment. The core model calls for examination of early job characteristics, attitudes, and their interrelationship; intermediate work experiences and attitudes; and finally later job characteristics. More precise discussion of the core model follows.

Early Period

Upon termination of formal schooling, whether the circumstances be favorable or unfavorable, most young people obtain employment at varying levels of occupational status and wage rates.[1] They will also remain with the initial employment for varying periods of time. The first job is likely to produce a variety of attitudinal reactions, many of which are likely to be dependent on the quality of that first job. For example, if the work is incidental or "secondary" in character, reactions are likely to be unfavorable. Other attitudes are formed prior to the work itself, although they certainly are affected by the first job. Whether the young person works out of an intrinsic or extrinsic motivation is an important concern, for example, but just as important might be whether that motivation finds a match in the character of the first job. A young person also brings career aspirations to an initial work experience and oftentimes these aspirations are determined relative to the status of that first job. Both initial job experiences and attitudes affect the level of satisfaction from that early employment experience. In particular, more favorable job characteristics in terms of higher occupational

1. An increasingly attractive option for youth is to obtain their initial job experience while in school. This study, however, only considers postschool experience. For insight into in-school vocational experiences and their effects on later employment, readers might consult Grasso and Shea (1979).

status and wages and usually longer tenure positively affect intrinsic motivation, which in turn or separately or even in interaction positively relates to job satisfaction. As an initial job characteristic, tenure is more problematic than status and wages since its presence does not necessarily indicate positive attitudes but rather perhaps economic or psychological insecurity.

Finally, a negative relationship is hypothesized between job characteristics and aspirations as those youth with low status jobs seek to escape from such a work environment by envisioning future enriched opportunities. Moreover, those youth with higher aspirations are less likely to be satisfied with their current job.

Middle Period

The experiences and attitudes from the early period carry over into the middle period. An important concern at this point is whether the youngster has stayed with the initial job or changed jobs. Further, has the level of satisfaction relative to the job changed and how has it been affected by job retention or job mobility? Certainly these considerations are largely affected by the nature of the initial job experience and the attitudes connected with it. Another concern in the middle period is whether the specific job attitudes from the early period get transformed into generalized dispositions toward work, expressed as a commitment to the work ethic. It is hypothesized that high quality first jobs with correspondent intrinsic motivation and positive satisfaction lead to job stability and mid-term satisfaction and commitment. Overly high aspirations, however, are proposed to lead to job mobility and dissatisfaction and lack of commitment.

Late Period

The late period contains the principal dependent variables of the study as the youth sample, now in its twenties or thirties, enters a more stable and hopefully more productive stage of its career. There are of course exceptions, for example as new entrants, particularly married women, come into the labor market or as people change jobs and careers. During this period, the analysis focuses on occupational level and wages at this career stage.

It is naturally expected that the first job itself directly affects later employment. Further, the attitudes produced by the first job are expected to have a combined or even separate effect on later work. The exception here is career aspirations which are thought at very high levels to be unrealistic, leading to frustrated opportunities. Medium, and therefore more realistic, career aspirations are hypothesized to lead to an optimal work situation in the late period.

The middle period, although affected by first job experiences and attitudes, has direct effects on later employment as well. Job stability and satisfaction are positively related to work experience. Moreover, it is hypothesized that the generalized work attitudes of the middle period, which were generated over time from the more specific job attitudes of the early period, are critical in explaining later employment. In order to prosper in ultimate worklife, one must have a commitment to the work ethic as opposed to a feeling that one gets ahead solely through luck or coincidence.

Full Model

The core model specifies a set of longitudinal interrelationships among work-related variables which, in and of themselves, contribute to a theory of initial job experiences and later employment. However, they are not expected to account for most of the variance in later work conditions since there are obviously a variety of demographic, educational, and labor market factors which affect career development apart from work experiences. Since the core model essentially represents an average of career developments of various subgroups of the youth population, as represented by these exogenous factors, its analysis can change for any subgroup chosen. Naturally, variation from the average pattern will not be uniform; rather, some subgroup categories will show marked between-group and within-group differences in their early career experience. It is expected, for example, that large differences will be found for both sex and race categories. Other demographic factors to be considered are age, socioeconomic status, and marital status, in addition to educational and intelligence categories. The economic environment of work, for example, the period in the business cycle and the place and region of employment, will also be more closely examined.

These exogenous factors obviously affect more than simply the end-points of the analysis—the later work characteristics; they indeed can affect conditions at every stage of career development. For example, the first job takes place in a particular economic environment and its quality is largely affected by family and educational background. Initial attitudes and aspirations are also affected by background, as are mid-term experiences and attitudes. For instance, a young married woman earning a second family income or a worker in a tight labor market with many vacancies might be more prone to change jobs in the middle period than other types of workers. Or, a youngster with a good world of work knowledge is likely to have reasonable career aspirations and, if he or she can locate a relatively responsible and promising first job, is also likely to be more satisfied with that job than someone lacking such knowledge. At this point, the model can become very complex as the number of interrelationships becomes a multiplicative function of the number of newly introduced exogenous variables. However, by superimposing these variables on the core model through separate subgroup analyses or through general multiple regression analysis, the significant antecedents of the core model can be isolated and incorporated. A full model explaining the relative role of initial job experiences in conjunction with environmental preconditions in accounting for later employment can then be revealed.

Complete detail on the core model, including description of the sample, the variables, and the analysis used, is provided in chapter 3. Theoretical background for the model incorporating a review of three literatures—that of sociology, economics, and psychology—is furnished in chapter 2. The results of the analysis of the core model, which are discussed on the basis of path analysis and separate subgroup analyses, are provided in chapter 4, which concludes with the presentation of the full model of initial job experiences. Finally, in chapter 5, the results are summarized and implications are drawn for public policy on youth employment.

Chapter 2
Review of the Youth Career Literature

While the number of studies which present various aspects of the model described in chapter 1 number in the thousands, only a handful undertake the comprehensive, longitudinal perspective which has been delineated. Nevertheless, the numerous micro and cross-sectional studies have made important contributions to the development of an integrated theory of initial job experiences such as the one proposed here.

Previous research in this area seems to fall into three principal classifications:

(1) studies which trace sociological and economic precursors of early and later work experience;

(2) psychological studies which detail specific predictors of job attitudes, such as job involvement and job satisfaction, the latter of which for example has recognized links to later work experience;

(3) studies which begin to explore the significance of early career attitudes and experiences in terms of subsequent employment.

In order to establish the placement of this study in the context of this large body of research, this chapter will outline the principal contributions according to the three classifications stated above.

Sociological and Economic Precursors

A rich body of sociological literature substantiates the importance of family background on subsequent work, in spite of a continuing belief in our society in the Protestant work ethic or in Algerism—opportunities afforded to all by a free society. In 1962, Simpson and Harper (1962) found the tendency for men to inherit the occupational status levels of their fathers to be persistent in our society. Blau and Duncan (1967), in their ambitious national sample survey, found that one-third of the variation in the socioeconomic ranking of the first job for young men is explained by their own educational attainment in combination with the education and occupation of their fathers. They further reported that this same first job accounts for a third of the differences in the ranking of their later jobs.

The so-called "status attainment model" in sociological research (Duncan, Featherman, and Duncan 1972; Sewell and Hauser 1975) essentially visualizes job placement in the way depicted above. A youth certainly has some choice in selecting a job, but that choice is invariably influenced by the socioeconomic status of the parents, the aspirations they instill in the youngster, and the education they are able to provide. Maizels (1970), in her comprehensive study of British school leavers, found this social class effect to be particularly strong for boys as opposed to girls, although the effect did hold for girls as well. Freestone (1939) explained that the reason for this relationship is that children tend to aim at the highest level available to the group to which they belong.

Researchers involved in the Career Thresholds study (see Parnes et al. 1970; Zeller et al. 1970; Kohen and Parnes 1971; and Kohen and Andrisani 1973), examining the young male cohort of the National Longitudinal Surveys, explained further that older, better educated individuals from wealthier families had superior labor market knowledge, had higher educational and occupational expectations, obtained more education, and went on to get better jobs with higher pay.

Throughout the Career Thresholds study and in both prior and subsequent studies, it should be noted that job quality is measured typically by both occupational prestige and income. Job changing (Maizels 1970; Baxter 1975), however, serves as a separate dependent variable. Nevertheless, similar sociological traits to those reported above have been found to be the most powerful predictors. Carter (1962) pinpointed I.Q. as an additional and major contributory factor, but Duncan, Featherman, and Duncan (1972) later disclosed that measures of intelligence do not significantly improve the predictive power of models of job quality which seem to depend heavily on the traditional predictors of educational attainment and family background. Duncan, Featherman, and Duncan (1972) as well as Sewell, Haller, and Ohlendorf (1970) and Porter (1974), although making a case for the inclusion of motivational measures in these models, also have found little incremental variance explained by including motivation. Baxter (1975), in interpreting Maizels' (1970) finding that job changing among young men was more frequent in smaller sized firms, suggested that training, which is offered commonly in large firms, may be a discriminating factor.

Whatever number of independent measures have been accumulated to explain job quality, sociologists have not been satisfied with the amount of explained variance. Indeed, Jencks et al. (1972) attributed a great deal of explanation of status and income to "luck," or factors beyond the individual's control. However, in Jencks' recent study, *Who Gets Ahead?,* Yankelovich (1979) reports that Jencks and his colleagues, using a broader range of surveys and variables, have essentially come back to support the familiar measures. Particularly vis-a-vis occupational status, as much as 75 percent of the variance can be explained by family background, test scores, educational attainment, and teenage personality traits.

Inherent in Jencks' and earlier studies pointing to the impact of family background, race is a principal predictor. Not only are blacks, as the single most studied minority group, handicapped because of family background, but also in spite of it (Blau and Duncan 1967). Piker (1968), in a comprehensive literature review, reported that a disproportionately large number of black youth come from lower status families. Beyond this social class impediment, blacks also face, according to Piker, the problem of racial discrimination and its attendant effects on self-image and personal motivation. However, job expectations of blacks may be higher, equal to, or lower than those of whites, depending upon a multitude of complex factors.

Ornstein (1976), using a retrospective longitudinal design in his entry study of a national sample of American men, made some interesting discoveries to advance knowledge of labor force entry and ultimate employment experience. He found that marital status has an impact upon later work in the sense that married men display considerably less mobility than single men. He also found that pre-entry work experiences have little long term impact. His corroboration of earlier findings reported here are also interesting due to their level of complexity afforded by path analytic and multivariate models. For example, he found that educational attainment, which in itself accounts for much of the influence of family background, has a stronger effect on prestige than wages. This is one reason, he concludes, why blacks are in a relatively worse position in terms of prestige than they are in terms of wages; their lower levels of education have less impact on wages. Finally, in terms of isolating any independent effects of the first job on later work experience, Ornstein shows that this effect is large on a job held eight years later, but much of the effect can be traced back to family background and education.

The contribution of economic theory to initial job choice and ultimate employment has been significant. Classical economists, as reported by Rottenberg (1956), believe that people make occupational choices in terms of relative prices in different occupations. In terms of macroeconomic impact on job choice, then, it is reasonable to assume that a worker will accept a low wage in present employment at the trough of the business cycle because he has a low estimation of his future earnings prospects if he should leave to search for an alternative. On the other hand, in periods of cyclical peak when opportunities for work elsewhere are plentiful and there is high expectation of long-run earnings, a worker will be less likely to accept a low wage.

Another tradition in economic thought, known as human capital theory, has parallels to the status attainment model in sociological inquiry. According to its architects (see, e.g., Becker 1964 or Thurow 1969), future employment, especially earnings, arises from prior employment experience as well as from formal education. Youth make a series of decisions in their early careers which have relative value to them as employees. They can search aggressively for a good job or take one near at hand, build up tenure on the same job or drift aimlessly from job to job, join a union or abstain from membership, and stay in school or drop out. These decisions, or investments in human capital, can have direct payoffs in terms of later work experience.

The classical and human capital theories, however, have come under attack over the years. For example, it has been pointed out that workers' knowledge of competitive wage and nonwage terms of employment is meager; therefore, there is no reason to assume a purposeful movement of workers among jobs (Reynolds 1948). Further, due to dissatisfaction among workers (Blauner 1964; *Work in America* 1973) as well as to institutional barriers as characterized by the dual labor market theorists (Doeringer and Piore 1971; Gordon 1971, 1972; Harrison 1971, 1972; Cain 1975), there are known limitations to the decisions that youth can make. The dual labor market theory asserts, for example, that regardless of skills, disadvantaged workers shift endlessly from job to job and are denied access to good jobs with the usual benefits and due process as a result of discrimination.

The actual behavior of people vis-a-vis job choice is, in real life, probably somewhere in between the conclusions of the classicists and so-called neo-classicists. Differences in wages will tend gradually, over time, to encourage greater mobility. However, it is also likely that due to institutional or informational barriers, wage and prestige differentials will remain but tend towards an equilibrium at which the total demand for each category of labor exactly matches its competitive supply (Samuelson 1972: Part IV).

With the advent of more sophisticated empirical research, it has been shown that cyclical conditions are not associated with real wage reduction or expansion in all occupations and industries. In particular, such industries as the services, which are somewhat immune to cyclical swings, have expanded regardless of cyclical swings (Gilroy 1973). Nevertheless, there is ample evidence that, on the whole, cyclical labor market factors account for some variation in first job selection, behavior, and attitudes.

Other demographic factors such as area and region of residence are also known to play an important role in occupational achievement (Jones 1967). Concentration in white-collar jobs (mostly clerical and sales) is heavy in metropolitan areas, particularly in the central cities, for example. However, large central cities have experienced a decline in recent years in such areas as manufacturing, wholesale and retail trade, and construction, which unfortunately incorporate a fruitful source of job opportunities for the young and the poor. Such jobs are moving to the suburbs. Remaining in the central cities are the office, financial, service, and government activities (Netzer 1970). Nonmetropolitan areas traditionally afford greater concentrations of blue-collar and farm jobs (Fremon 1970).

Although region of residence is known to affect wage levels, its impact upon early and subsequent occupational choice is open to question. Westcott (1976) found that occupational differences by race stem, to a great extent, from geographical differences rather than from other considerations. Andrisani et al. (1977), however, attribute little significance to regional differences in accounting for career aspirations.

The Psychological Focus on Job Satisfaction

The psychological literature on youth careers addresses the attitudes developed during or caused by early job experiences, as well as attitudes resulting from more structural characteristics, such as environmental preconditions. These attitudes, important in explaining behavior (Kiesler, Collins, and Miller 1969), are also known to shape subsequent work experience. Before reviewing this latter set of relationships, it is important to consider the antecedents of job attitudes. Studies along this line seem to focus on two psychological constructs, job satisfaction and job involvement. Literally thousands of studies have attempted to define these similar constructs and to discover the factors which affect them (Saleh and Hosek 1976; Rabinowitz and Hall 1977; Aldag and Brief 1978).

In this section a survey of the job satisfaction literature is provided,[1] to be followed in the next section by an examination of the consequences of this specific attitude as well as the consequences of more generalized career attitudes on later work experience. Researchers generally agree that the most appropriate approach to the discussion of the antecedents of job satisfaction is one that takes into consideration two basic aspects: the characteristics of the job itself and the personal characteristics which the individual brings to the job.

Effects of Job Characteristics

Job characteristics which have been shown to influence job satisfaction include wage levels, promotional opportunities, supervisory behavior, job content, job level and status, organizational structure and size of company, interaction with peers, and physical conditions. These variables have been found to have disparate effects upon satisfaction. In *The Motivation to Work,* Herzberg, Mausner, and Snyderman (1959) explained the impact of some of these variables by using Maslow's need hierarchy to formulate the motivator/hygiene theory of employee motivation. Variables affecting job satisfaction were divided into two sets of factors: job intrinsic factors (such as achievement, recognition, responsibility, advancement, the work itself) were labelled "motivators," or satisfiers; job extrinsic

1. For the purpose of this review, job satisfaction and job involvement are treated as identities. Some researchers, i.e., Lodahl and Kejner (1965) or Weissenberg and Gruenfeld (1968), have discouraged this kind of treatment although the former researchers found both constructs to have roughly the same factorial content.

factors (such as supervision, security, working conditions, company policy and administration, interpersonal relationships) were labelled "hygiene factors," or dissatisfiers. According to the theory:

> the presence of "motivators" at satisfactory levels in the employee's job will lead to job satisfaction. However, the absence of "motivators" will not lead to job dissatisfaction . . . It is the "hygienes" whose absence from satisfactory levels of fulfillment may lead to job dissatisfaction, but the presence of satisfactory fulfillment of "hygienes" in the job situation will not lead to job satisfaction, but a neutral state (Kaplan, Tausky, and Bolaria 1969: 792).

Herzberg's research provided the basis for a great deal of further study. Hulin and Waters (1971) observed that intrinsic factors are more important than extrinsic factors in determining overall job satisfaction. However, many researchers have obtained results conflicting with those of Herzberg. A study by Turner and Lawrence (1965) demonstrated that certain effects on job satisfaction, particularly among workers of different cultural backgrounds, were more complex than could be explained by the simple motivator/hygiene model. In general, it has been reported that while people do distinguish among the various aspects of a job and can make separate evaluative judgments about them, it is difficult to sort out the independent effects of these components on overall satisfaction (Kahn 1974).

The many studies of the effect of wage level upon job satisfaction generally show a relationship between high pay and high satisfaction. Lawler and Porter (1963) demonstrated this in a study of job satisfaction among 2,000 managers where it was found that satisfaction was related to wage level when managerial level was held constant.

The effect of organizational structure upon job attitudes was observed in a study by Newman (1975), who found that employees' attitudes were related to the objective characteristics of their location, both physical and hierarchical, within an organization. The type of supervision an employee receives is also an important determinant of job satisfaction.

Job content has been found to be one of the most important components of job satisfaction. Research has shown that simple, routine, non-challenging jobs often lead to high employee dissatisfaction, to increased absenteeism and turnover, and to substantial difficulties in effectively managing employees who work on simplified jobs (Hackman and Lawler 1971). Workers most frequently cite fractionation and lack of control, or to put it in positive terms, variety and autonomy as the most important factors of job content that affect satisfaction (Kahn 1974).

Job level and the status attached to that level have also been thought to be related to job satisfaction (Tannenbaum 1966). Lodahl and Kejner (1965) and Rabinowitz (1975) investigated job level as a predictor of job involvement, and Mannheim (1975) as a predictor of "centrality." Further research by Kavanagh and Halpern (1977) found that persons in higher level jobs did not experience greater satisfaction in their lives because of higher pay and status. This finding reflects the evidence that individual differences in achievement motivation and aspiration play a crucial role in job satisfaction. For example, some researchers have concluded that people with high need for achievement will be more dissatisfied regardless of how high a job level they have reached. Therefore, while it is important to understand which of the components of a job may have a bearing upon employee satisfaction, a mere description of the effects of these variables does little to explain why these effects take place or why these variables have varying effects upon individuals. Thus, researchers have addressed themselves to examining differential interpretations which workers may attach to a particular job situation, the varying desires and aspirations of different levels of workers, and differences in values among workers (Kasl 1974).

This contingency perspective has accompanied other studies of job characteristics and job satisfaction, and has led to a research focus on job satisfaction as a product of the person-environment interaction (MacEachron 1975, 1977). Hackman and Lawler (1971) initiated the famous need-strength studies which attempted to apply higher-order need satisfaction as a moderator of job level and satisfaction. Brief and Aldag (1975) followed up with a study of correction employees which essentially made the point that for optimum results, the psychological demands of the job must be matched to the personal needs of workers. Research on leader behavior (Jones, James, and Bruni 1975) and participation in decisionmaking (Siegel and Ruh 1973) employed similar interactive components.

Effects of Personal Characteristics

The impact of different personal characteristics of workers on job satisfaction has received perhaps more attention than job characteristics. Some of the variables examined have included age, tenure, sex, race, level of education, geographical background, marital status, perception of work, level of aspirations, preference for economic or noneconomic rewards, and acceptance of middle-class norms.

Of the above list of individual traits, age has received a fair amount of treatment with reasonably good results in its explanatory power (Schwyart and Smith 1972; Altimus and Tersine 1973; Jones, James, and Bruni 1975; Hall and Mansfield 1975). The principal contention is that older workers tend to become more satisfied with their job, have a better attendance record and less turnover, and identify themselves more strongly with management and its policies. Herzberg et al. (1957) noted the phenomenon of a U-shaped relationship between employee age, tenure, and job satisfaction, with high job satisfaction reported immediately upon beginning work, declining in the late twenties and thirties, and subsequently rising. Gibson and Klein (1970) suggested that age and tenure must be considered separately, however, as they found "a linear positive relationship between employee satisfaction and age and a linear negative relationship between employee satisfaction and length of service," slopes which in combination essentially form the U-shaped design. One explanation for the negative relationship between tenure and job satisfaction reported by Dubin and Porter (1974) is that entry level job incumbents evaluate their present situation more in terms of rewards (pay, prestige, power, etc.) than costs (effort, frustration, discomfort, etc.). Studies by Hulin and Smith (1965) and Hunt and Saul (1975) disputed the findings of Gibson and Klein by displaying that both age and company tenure had significant positive relationships to job satisfaction. Hulin and Smith postulated that their findings were due to the individual's ability over time to better adjust his expectations to what the job environment requires. Hunt and Saul warned of the difficulty of obtaining a simple explanation for any relationship among these variables due to the confounding effects of personality and situational variables.

Differences in male and female attitudes toward work have been observed in several studies. Hunt and Saul (1975) reported in their age and tenure study that overall job satisfaction was found to be more strongly associated with age than with tenure for males, whereas the opposite held true for females. There was, in fact, no evidence of a significant relationship of any kind between age and the overall satisfaction of females. Brayfield and Wells (1957) examined the degree of association between job and life satisfaction among men and women and reported a significant positive relationship only for men. In a hypothesis later elaborated upon by Siegel (1971), they speculated that the fact that work was thought to be more important in the lives of men caused this finding. Rabinowitz (1975) found higher average job involvement for men than women in a Canadian government ministry, but when the effects of job level and tenure were removed, sex differences disappeared. Further, a more recent study by Kavanagh and Halpern (1977) revealed that women are now reporting strong and significant relationships between job and life satisfaction, and the researchers hypothesized that this result might be attributed to changes in attitudes wrought by the women's movement.

Jones et al. (1977) examined varying perceptions of work and degrees of job satisfaction between black and white workers. They noted that while studies comparing blacks and whites have reported that blacks have higher occupational aspirations but lower job expectations, are less oriented toward planning for the future, and have a lower degree of achievement orientation, these findings could be attributed to several factors such as differences in frames of reference or differing work conditions between black and white workers. Their study of the job satisfaction of 4,315 U.S. Navy personnel revealed that when comparison of black and white sailors was restricted to individuals in the same organizational subsystems, many of the expected race-related differences vanished. Differences which did emerge depicted black sailors as having more positive attitudes which appeared to reflect lower needs rather than differences in perceived work conditions.

The relationship between education and job satisfaction has been studied by a number of researchers (Gurin, Veroff, and Feld 1960; Mannheim 1975; Jones, James, and Bruni 1975) with results being mixed. Siegel and Ruh (1973) found that education moderated the relationship between job involvement and participation in decisionmaking. Rabinowitz and Hall (1977) suggested that corrections for restriction of range may help clarify the relationship between education and job attitudes.

Marital status as a predictor of job satisfaction has received little attention, although Gannon and Hendrickson (1973) have answered the question of whether a person with family responsibilities will devote energies to work by presenting evidence showing that it is possible to be involved in both job and family.

On the basis of often cited studies by Turner and Lawrence (1965), Blood and Hulin (1967), and Hulin and Blood (1968), it has been speculated that community size is negatively related to job satisfaction. The reason provided in these studies for the negative relationship is the moderator concept of "alienation from middle-class norms." Workers from rural areas and small communities are hypothesized to be inculcated with middle-class norms, that is, to have personal involvement with their jobs, to have aspirations within their occupation, and basically to have goals of upward mobility. On the other hand, workers from urbanized communities are hypothesized to be at the opposite pole of the construct, to be only instrumentally involved in their jobs and to have only extraoccupational goals. The moderator concept notwithstanding, Siegel and Ruh (1973) found the relationship between urban background and job involvement to be positive.

Consequences of Early Career Attitudes and Experiences

With the advent of more sophisticated computer applications for treating multivariate data, researchers have begun the task of tracing the employment effects of job satisfaction and other early career attitudes and experiences.

Turning first to job satisfaction, it has been widely believed that there is a link between job satisfaction and job performance, if not directly, then through motivation. Nevertheless, reviews by Brayfield and Crockett (1955), Vroom (1964), and Schwab and Cummings (1970) have challenged this relationship. In fact, Lawler and Porter (1967) have explicitly postulated that the reverse ordering may be more correct.

Job dissatisfaction has received separate treatment as a deterrent to employment success. There is some substantiation, for example, for its relationship to turnover and absenteeism (Wickert 1951; Patchen 1965; Farris 1971; and Siegel and Ruh 1973). It is also thought to result in lower earnings, lack of interest in further education and training, and reduced aspirations. At the macro level, there has been increasing concern about job dissatisfaction because of its hypothesized effect on the quality of life (*Work in America* 1973; Hackman and Suttle 1977) and on alienation (Blauner 1964).

Andrisani et al. (1977), using all four cohorts of the National Longitudinal Surveys, specifically examined the relationship between job dissatisfaction and later employment. By regressing seven aspects of labor market experience (variables included turnover, change in occupational status, change in earnings, unemployment, labor force participation, completion of formal occupational training, and geographic mobility) on job dissatisfaction three to five years earlier, while holding other human capital variables constant, they were able to discern the subsequent costs of job dissatisfaction. The findings revealed that for each of the eight age-sex-race groups of the NLS there was a strong relationship between job dissatisfaction and turnover. The relationship was found to be more pronounced among younger than older workers and among blacks than whites. Further, there was evidence that dissatisfaction resulted in subsequent increased unemployment, decreased labor force participation, and below-average growth in both annual earnings and promotions. The only exception to this latter finding was for dissatisfied black workers who, compared to satisfied black workers, experienced greater occupational advancement largely as a result of their greater tendency to change employers.

Perhaps antecedent to job satisfaction and dissatisfaction in terms of effect on subsequent work experience are predispositions that workers develop as psychological reactions to work. There is some evidence, for example, that individuals may lean to certain jobs because of attitudes developed during childhood (Carter 1966; Kohn and Schooler 1973). McCall and Lawler (1976) studied such career attitudes or expectations among high school students and found that high school students from all backgrounds clearly distinguished between executive positions and assembly line jobs in terms of job satisfaction and of the likelihood of holding such job themselves. This initial orientation, they suggested, may be one reason why individuals who work in factory type jobs generally report lower job dissatisfaction than employees in higher prestige occupations. McCall and Lawler also traced sociological antecedents of preemployment attitudes and concluded that race and social class effects operate through the transmission of parental values and occupational experience, as well as through the child's awareness and beliefs about discrimination and job opportunities. They recommended further longitudinal study of job expectations.

Berryman (1978), in a youth unemployment study, revealed that youth displayed positive attitudes toward work and in fact possessed values and attitudes similar to adults prior to entry into the labor market. However, disenchantment sets in when these younger workers find that they are relegated to low-level jobs, leading in many cases to a selection of unemployment as an alternative to work.

The dissonance produced by unmet job expectations works in a vicious cycle with job experience, as Goodwin reports (1972):

> In the course of social experiences which include family interactions, early schooling, and subsequent contact with the work world itself, people not only are guided by their own work orientations but also undergo experiences that affect their orientations. That is, orientations are part of a feedback process in which the orientations influence action and then are themselves influenced by the action.

Some of the British studies referred to earlier support Goodwin's conclusion. Maizels (1970), for example, found that youth developed work expectations and aspirations while still in school, but that this development extended well into their first years at work, including the period of adjustment to working life. One difference between those who had remained in their first job and those who had held more than one job was revealed when the differences between their present jobs and their original preferences were examined. Twice as many, proportionately, of the boys with more than one job were in work which was quite different from that originally hoped for, as were boys with only one job. Baxter

(1975) further reported that those who were chronic job changers between the ages of fifteen and seventeen continued to change jobs between eighteen and twenty at a rate which was still well above the average. The frequent job changing established early in their working lives may have established a pattern for their future careers.

Finally, focusing on career aspirations, Andrisani et al. (1977) showed that youth with greater aspirations advanced more in annual earnings in subsequent years than comparable youth who were less ambitious. However, the findings for white youth were found to be largely attributable to their having higher status jobs initially. Nevertheless, for blacks the longitudinal analysis clearly established the effect of attitudes over subsequent behavior. Further, for both white and black youth, confidence in obtaining career goals was found to lead to greater subsequent success in the labor market during the transitional period from school to work.

In spite of these findings displaying attitudinal effects on subsequent work experience, there is ample evidence that initial jobs are the key to subsequent labor market behavior. Workers entering the labor market must reconcile their career goals with the opportunities realistically available to them. Disadvantaged workers, due to a history of social deprivation, have become the subject of much research along these lines. The disadvantaged have essentially learned to live with reduced needs and impoverished satisfaction (Wolfbein 1967). When exposed to satisfying work experiences, disadvantaged workers are able to retain some positive career aspirations. Wolfbein (1967) reported in a study of 100 disadvantaged participants in the Norfolk project, an experimental demonstration project established under the Manpower Development and Training Act, that there was an attempt to determine why some participants rejected training opportunities. While rejecters resembled accepters in age, educational attainment, marital status and wage level, the explanation of why the small training allowance was a deterrent in one case and not in the others seems to have derived from the difference in work experience. Rejecters were less likely to have acquired some sophistication toward employment opportunities as a result of training in military service or work outside the Norfolk-Plymouth area.

Work experiences of disadvantaged workers also affect their future employment because, as is reported by the dual labor market theorists (Doeringer and Dunlop 1969), accustomed to low wages, dead-end employment, undesirable working conditions and inequitable supervision, the disadvantaged worker often develops both working habits and expectations about jobs that are incompatible with the performance norms of higher wage enterprises.

Differences between the work orientations of the poor and the nonpoor have been attributed by researchers to the poor's adaptation to the situational facts of life and employment; they do not reflect cultural differences. A 1972 study by the Brookings Institution reported in Berg (1974: 32) demonstrated that the poor possess work orientations similar to those of middle-class Americans and accept public assistance only after they have experienced serious occupational failures. These failures the researchers found attributable to labor market conditions. A study of 30 underemployed black men in the District of Columbia (Goodwin 1972) further revealed that while they attached little importance to work, these men had only been able to obtain unskilled, menial jobs and had repeatedly failed in the work world.

Early or first job studies are naturally not restricted to the disadvantaged or poor. Dunnette, Avery, and Banas (1973) surveyed 1,000 college graduates who worked for a large employer for less than four years to determine why some had stayed and others had left the company. Both groups reported that the first job with the company was one that severely frustrated their high hopes and expectations of opportunities to use their abilities. Those who stayed apparently moved into later job assignments that much more closely matched pre-employment expectations, whereas later assignments in the company for those who left evidently were seen merely as more of the same. In this case, dissatisfied workers were able to find more satisfying jobs by changing employers. Dunnette and his associates added, however, that unsatisfactory work experience for those locked into low-level positions could lead to an above-average rate of turnover and ultimately frustrate career aspirations.

Utilizing the young men cohort of the National Longitudinal Surveys, Parnes and Kohen (1975) went beyond Dunnette, Avery, and Banas by demonstrating that both the earnings and prestige of a youth's first postschool job were positively and significantly related to ultimate success in the labor market. Finally, Andrisani et al. (1977) supplied evidence to demonstrate that job dissatisfaction among workers results from real disparities in earnings and status among comparable workers. They went on to demonstrate that this dissatisfaction leads to subsequent wage and status disparities. They also established that more favorable work experience leads to more favorable work attitudes.

Having presented evidence that both early career attitudes and early career experiences affect the quality of subsequent employment, it would be useful to know what their relative effects are or perhaps how they get integrated during the course of labor market experience. Need-strength theorists, as has been pointed out earlier, supposedly provide a link by proposing that job satisfaction, and consequently job success, result from a correspondence between the needs of the individual and the characteristics of the job. Expectancy theory essentially argues the same point (Hackman and

Lawler 1971). To the extent conditions of work can be arranged so that employees can satisfy their own needs by working effectively toward organizational goals, employees will in fact tend to work hard toward achievement of those goals.

Nevertheless, recent reviews of need-strength theories (Salancik and Pfeffer 1978; White 1979) unfortunately present conflicting evidence, placing into question the very utility of this entire body of theory. Consequently, alternative formulations have been proposed. Schein (1971), Van Maanen and Katz (1976), and Katz (1978) propose that the career or job longevity serves as a moderator of the job and respective response patterns. In other words, expectations about work and the job in particular differ during the course of an individual's career. Such a formulation contrasts with a theory of the importance of the first job. Salancik and Pfeffer (1978) also question the value of need-strength theory in their social information process model. They posit that multiple social influences at work affect attitudes much more than individual needs or other characteristics. Workers possess the ability to construct their own satisfaction by selectively perceiving and interpreting their social environment. Therefore, workers adapt to different work situations and are influenced as much by past behavior and social effects as by needs or job characteristics at a particular point in time.

These new formulations notwithstanding, a vast number of studies in this area (White 1979) do show positive relationships between job quality and worker response. This perhaps serves to confirm the contentions of the original human relations theorists (see, for example, Argyris 1957; McGregor 1960; Likert 1967). Argyris argues that nonhumanistic management systems and work conditions produce regressive organizations which resist change and result in workers' withdrawal, passivity, and feelings of psychological failure. In a way, Argyris agrees with Salancik and Pfeffer that workers adapt to their job environments; however, if the environment is insufficiently stimulating and challenging, they will become nonresponsive to the job's task characteristics. Therefore, early job experiences are crucial in developing positive worker responses, although bad early experiences can be reversed through job redesign or worker movement to improved work settings.

Another formulation regarding the relative effects of early career attitudes and experiences is to view attitudes, as Doob (1947) suggested, as intervening between the objective stimulus—the job—and the ultimate response—the subsequent work preference. Job satisfaction is proposed in this study to be too immediate to serve as a transferring agent to subsequent experience. Therefore, attitudes describing general work dispositions seem more appropriate. This contention arises from a distinction between the concepts of "job" and "work," as supplied by social psychologists. Job is more definable in terms of objective, external criteria whereas work is seen as being dependent on the individual's personality, approach to life, or individuality (Tiffany, Cowan, and Tiffany 1974). Therefore, attitudes toward work incorporate more of a commitment than immediate job attitudes, and, in behavioral terms, are essentially generalizable from cues emanating from first and subsequent jobs and the attitudes associated with them, including job satisfaction.

As early as 1944, in Lewin's aspiration level studies (Lewin et al. 1944), it was found that people tend to raise their level of aspiration following successful goal attainment. Hall and Nougaim (1968) identified a "success syndrome," and Bray, Campbell, and Grant (1974) found that success breeds greater involvement in subsequent work. Dubin et al. (1975) discussed the importance of a "central life interest" in work in determining a worker's level of commitment to his work organization. They noted that workers who incorporate a centrality of an institution into their overall orientation tended to view their current work environment through a filter which leads to a high level of commitment and makes many features of the environment appear attractive regardless of their objective attractiveness.

Another way to view this notion of general work attitudes as intervening between early and later job experiences is to consider cognitive models of attitude change, in particular the concepts of consistency and dissonance. The tendency towards consistency is considered to be one of the main characteristics of human thought, behavior, and action (Halloran 1967). Cognitions tend to be integrated by people in order to provide meaning and stability in everyday experience. New information can disrupt this integrated state, producing dissonance. According to Festinger (1957), people will tend to do whatever is easiest to achieve consistency and avoid dissonance. Some cognitive psychologists believe that a little bit of dissonance is good for the individual in that it relieves boredom (Hunt 1963). However, others assume that consistency or congruity is the desired comfortable state of an organism (Osgood and Tannenbaum 1955). In fact, some individuals, in order to resist change, will selectively expose themselves to information which confirms rather than distorts their original attitudes. This process has been viewed psychoanalytically as a mechanism of ego defense to ward off the reality of existing dangers (Sarnoff 1960).

Given this background, it is conceivable that the first job of a youth produces a responsive attitude which is significant enough in the youth's total experience to become imprinted, or in cognitive terminology, to serve as a base for consistency. This job attitude can become generalized into an overall attitude towards work unless changes in the environment (i.e., a new job) or other conditions produce sufficient dissonance to change the original attitude. Although extensive research has been done in the area of cognitive dissonance, it is not clear in the work environment how easy it is to change an attitude. It is known, however, that behavior is harder to change than an attitude, particularly when the behavior contains a commitment which is relatively irrevocable (Malewski 1964). A question remains, then, as to whether the first job is of sufficient impact to sustain an ultimate commitment to work (or lack thereof).

Finally, internal-external attitudes (Rotter 1966), particularly the degree to which individuals perceive success at work as the product of personal initiative or luck, are also thought to be important in explaining some of the variance in subsequent work experience. Runyon (1973) and Reitz and Jewell (1979) have found positive relationships between locus of control (another way to describe these general internal-external attitudes) and job involvement, the latter suggesting that this relationship is particularly strong for males. With respect to effects on subsequent work experience, Andrisani et al. (1977), although at the time of their study having limited data on the young men cohort and none for the young women, did find that younger men, both white and black, with an internal outlook were in higher status occupations and had higher hourly earnings two years later than comparable externals. The only aspect of labor market experience examined that was not significantly related to prior internality/externality was growth in annual earnings, much of which might have been accounted for by investments by young internals in human capital, i.e., education.

Although it has been contended that work attitudes, conceivably produced by early job experiences, essentially act as transferring agents to later work experience, it is also conceivable that such attitudes may not have much staying power due to changes that workers make from job to job. These job changes may affect one's job satisfaction which could disrupt the formation of a consistent work attitude.

Given the research that has been done, something is known about who in fact changes jobs. Among youth, certainly the younger ones are more prone to change (Blau and Duncan 1967; Zeller et al. 1970), as are those with a higher degree of education (Ornstein 1976). In addition, whites, those in lower occupational categories, and those who are dissatisfied with their initial job(s) are more likely to engage in job transitions (Kohen et al. 1977; Andrisani et al. 1977). Reasons for mobility differ somewhat depending upon the category examined, but the overall rationale is economic; and, in fact, individuals who make job changes normally derive economic if not occupational benefits. Further, there is some evidence that mobility produces greater job satisfaction (Kohen et al. 1977), and that dissatisfied youth, apart from white men, can advance career-wise more than their satisfied counterparts if they make a job change (Andrisani et al. 1977).

Work To Be Done

Throughout the review above, it should be apparent that few studies are available (Ornstein 1976 and Schmitt et al. 1978, representing exceptions) which attempt to connect in a path model multiple determinants of a youth's subsequent work experience. Further, the relative contributions of sociological, economic, and psychological factors are unknown. There is also a need for longitudinal analysis of these factors over a reasonably long period of time in order to demonstrate the relative participation of particular traits, attitudes, and behaviors not only over short periodic intervals, but over an entire segment of a youth's career.

Methodologically, a relatively large sample of the youth population is required in order to incorporate sufficient cases in categories from different demographic, educational, and labor market subgroups. This would permit the eventual application of exogenous controls on the model. Nevertheless, the sample should be restricted in its employment characteristics since relative uniformity on this feature would insure reliable identification of subsequent effects produced by initial job experiences. Finally, given the past emphasis on cross-sectional, correlational research, it now seems appropriate to move to specification of a causal model of initial job experiences and later employment so that the sequence of relationships inherent in the evolution of a youth's early career may be revealed.

Once a model has been specified, it would be essential that the ongoing research result in public policy interpretations that apply the knowledge gained to improvement in our society's youth employment.

Chapter 3
An Approach to Analysis of Early Youth Careers

Sample

The data base for this study is the National Longitudinal Surveys (NLS), a massive study of the labor market experience of four cohorts of the United States civilian population: men 45 to 59 years of age, women 30 to 44 years of age, and young men and women 14 to 24 years of age. For the purposes of this research, only the two youth cohorts were considered. Each cohort represents a national probability sample of approximately 5,000 individuals. To be exact, the original samples included 5,225 male respondents, and 5,159 female respondents.

The surveys were originally commissioned in 1965 by the Office of Manpower Policy, Evaluation, and Research of the U.S. Department of Labor under contract with the Center for Human Resource Research of The Ohio State University. The survey work, however, was performed by the Bureau of the Census, which was responsible for the design of the sample, the field work, and the data processing.

The NLS was primarily designed to analyze the sources of variation in the labor market behavior and experiences of the four separate cohorts. (For an extensive discussion of the NLS, see Parnes 1975.) Its longitudinal character has been instrumental to the type of research considered here because its tracking of individuals' job experiences has provided a basis for ascertaining patterns in people's careers over time. The data set is particularly appropriate for this study because it represents a source of early labor market information on young people whose characteristics, early job experiences, and attitudes generated by or apart from job experiences can be observed to see if they have any effect on subsequent employment experience.

The total sample of young men and young women was not used in this study since it represents individuals who have had dissimilar early labor market experiences in terms of such characteristics as number of jobs and tenure. Further, the total sample includes individuals who are still in school. Therefore, a subset of the sample had to be derived which would represent a correspondent group of people with regard to their early work experiences. The derivation of this subsample is described below, first for the young men, then for the young women.

The Young Men Subsample

The principal criterion for sample inclusion was that individuals be having "first" job experiences. The notion of "early" job experiences was thought to be too generalized and disperse (i.e., over what amount of jobs does one cease to have an early experience?). Therefore, it was felt that a focus on first job holders would produce a distinctive sample.

Turning to the young men, then, the total sample as indicated earlier contained 5,225 respondents with data available for the following years: 1966, 1967, 1968, 1969, 1970, 1971, 1973, and 1975. A subset of this sample was created by a selection procedure which narrowed membership to youngsters who were working on a first job but for no more than seven years and who were out of school.[1]

The baseline subsample included 743 cases. As might be expected, there is depreciation in the number of cases across time. For example, 728 individuals (15 missing) responded to a job satisfaction item in 1966, but only 546 (197 missing) responded to the same item presented in 1969. The subjective items, i.e., the attitudinal measures, appear to suffer the greatest depreciation across time. The responses to the more quantifiable job characteristic types of items are generally less susceptible to this decrement.

The Young Women Subsample

The total sample of young women included 5,159 respondents with data available for the following years: 1968, 1969, 1970, 1971, 1972, 1973, and 1975. As can be seen immediately, there was a two-year lag in the conduct of the young women's surveys as compared to the young men. The women's surveys began in 1968, whereas the men's surveys began in 1966. However, since the design of this research called for combining the male and female files, it was necessary to resolve the temporal discrepancy. One solution was to equate 1968 women variables with 1966 men variables as much as possible and to stagger the remaining variables accordingly two years apart. Technically speaking, this would have necessitated analyzing 1977 data on the women

1. The selection statement, incorporating the male subset membership conditions, was formulated as follows:

1) R's current (or last) job is his first job and the year he started the job was between 1960 and 1966;
2) R's current (or last) job in 1967 is not his first job and the year he started the first job since he stopped attending school was 1966 (only for those R's providing consistent responses during any or all of the years—1967, 1968, and/or 1969—that the questions were asked);
3) R's current job is the first job since he stopped attending high school.

as corresponding to the latest period on the men, collected in 1975. Unfortunately, the 1977 data for the young women were not available from the Center for Human Resource Research at the inception of the study. Therefore, a decision was made to consider 1968 women variables as early period variables, comparable to the 1966 variables for the men. Thereafter, for middle and later years, variables would be selected for identical years; for example, 1975 women variables would be combined with 1975 men variables. This procedure resulted in the total span for the young women being merely two years shorter than the young men. Given that the total span of time for the young men is nine years, a fair representation can be obtained for the young women's later period, even if the last year of data is in the seventh year.

With respect to subsample selection in the young women's file, the same conditions of membership as described in the previous section for the young men's file were observed with one exception. Since there was a two-year lag in the women's data, to provide for no more than a seven-year tenure on the first job, the year of first job variable was recorded for years 1962 to 1968, rather than 1960 to 1966 as it was applied to the men.[2]

The baseline subsample resulting from the selection procedure for the young women included 657 cases.

2. The selection statement for the young women subsample included two statements:

1) the year R started current job was between 1962 and 1968;
2) R's current job is the first job since she stopped attending high school.

The additional statement incorporated in formulating the men's file was omitted in the young women subsample preparation due to lack of data. There were other minor changes in the young women's selection statement because of data idiosyncracies; for example, the intersection of the "year of first job" and "is current job your first job" variables produced no cells in the case of the young women and is probably due to question sequencing. Nevertheless, it is believed that the young women subsample has comparable properties to the young men with respect to respondents being employed, out-of-school first job holders who have been on the job for no more than seven years.

File Consolidation

The young men and young women files were merged not only as a means to include sex as a variable in the study, but also to substantially increase the number of cases to be analyzed. The combined file contained 1,400 cases.

The file consolidation was made possible by identifying all the variables in the young women's data that were identical to those already comprising the young men's variable list. The temporal sequencing was accomplished by the procedure described earlier. As might be expected, some questions were presented differently to the male and the female samples, and some questions asked of the men were not found in the young women's questionnaire. Nevertheless, most male variables had female counterparts and were accordingly merged to produce the combined file which formed the data set for all subsequent analyses.

Sample Restrictions

Although this study has attempted to create a consistent subsample of young people, similar in their initial job experiences, a number of limitations bear mentioning. First, as was indicated earlier, respondents who were enrolled in school, whether part time or full time, whether working or not, were unfortunately excluded since they were not asked a number of relevant questions pertaining to this study. As a result, a significant drop in the usable number of cases occurred.

Also excluded, due to the NLS survey design, were those who were unemployed the week prior to the survey or those who were actively searching for work. This exclusion may have had unintentional consequences on some subsequent measures. For example, it is conceivable that the distribution of job satisfaction scores, which is highly skewed favoring positive responses, may have been more balanced had these two groups been asked the same job satisfaction question relative to their previous job.

Another issue which presents a shortcoming of the NLS data set in terms of response reliability concerns one of the principal conditions in the selection statement explained above for the male file. For those individuals whose current or last job was not their first, a probe question was asked as to the year they began their first job since leaving school. This question appeared in the 1967, 1968, and the 1969 surveys of young males. One would expect that regardless of when or how often that question was asked, a person's response would tend to be the same—the vast majority having had only one "first" job, with the possible exception of those few who quit work to attend school only to re-enter the labor force at some future date. There are, however, actually too few of these cases to account for an excessively large proportion of inconsistent responses. In a cross tabulation of the "year of first job" variables for the years 1967, 1968, 1969, by each other, between 42.8 percent and 49.1 percent of the cases were discovered residing in the off-diagonal cells of the tables. For example, when first asked in 1967 to state the year they started their first job since they stopped attending school, as compared with the same question asked in 1968, 45 R's answered in a consistent fashion while 16 did not. Of those 16 inconsistent cases, 10 were off by only one year. There were some cases, on the other hand, demonstrating much greater margins of error. In fact, for one case there was as much as a seven-year spread between responses from one year to the next on the same basic question.

As a result, in the subsample the author has constructed of first job holders, greater faith can be placed in the responses to the question, "Is your current job your first job . . ." than, "When did you start working at your first job since you stopped attending school?" The latter requires more exacting recall ability on the part of the respondent than does the simple yes/no response to the former question.[3]

Given the above conclusion, the ultimate subsample of cases selected for this study excluded most cases where inconsistent responses were evidenced in terms of the "year started first job" items. This hopefully has reduced error on the basis of recall inconsistency and suggests confidence in the validity of the relationships to be explored.

Attrition of Cases

As was mentioned above in the section on the young men subsample, the data, as is characteristic of longitudinal designs, suffer attrition in the number of cases across time. A question arises, therefore, as to whether to utilize the sample number of cases represented in the earliest period or whether to consider the number represented in the latest period. In this study, the dependent variables were assigned for the year 1975; namely, occupational status in 1975, and income from wages and salary in 1975. The wages item suffers a decrement of 633 cases, and the occupation item suffers a loss of 314 cases. Conducting analyses involving these and prior variables with the reduced number of nonmissing cases would have severely limited the scope of the study, particularly for subsequent subgroup analyses. Therefore, a decision was made to retain the 1,400 cases present at the earliest period: 1966 for the men and 1968 for the women.

This decision was based, further, on knowledge about attrition as supplied by prior NLS researchers (see, for exam-

3. A conversation held with Dr. Stephen Hills of the Center for Human Resource Research confirmed this conclusion. According to Dr. Hills, one might infer from these response patterns that those who have had unpleasant early experiences tend to selectively forget details about those early experiences. Although not an item to be used in this research, he reported that other researchers have had particular difficulties with recall of the question, "In what years were you enrolled in the high school you last attended?"

ple, Kohen et al. 1977: 4-5). Although losses are not randomly distributed (e.g., attrition is generally higher for blacks than for whites and varies by a number of characteristics within each racial group), variation in attrition is not very great, and one might therefore argue that missing respondents have characteristics similar to those who were successfully followed up.[4]

Variables

As was suggested earlier, the NLS data contain literally hundreds of variables treating such respondent characteristics as educational experience, current job information, work history, and social, psychological, and economic background. The research described here began with a careful filtering of this voluminous information in order to produce a manageable variable set conforming to the core model outlined in chapter 1. In particular, information was sought on initial job characteristics and career attitudes associated with first jobs, on intermediate work attitudes and experiences, and on later work experience. Information was also sought on respondent demographic and education characteristics as well as initial labor market conditions. These so-called exogenous variables were brought into the analysis subsequent to the treatment of the principal variables. Accordingly, the principal variables were arranged on a longitudinal basis; that is, they were separated into ear-

4. To examine this contention further, a comparative analysis was made of a zero-order correlation matrix containing all variables in the study, all of which either originally appeared as or were subsequently converted to measures approximating interval properties. Comparing the full subsample ($N = 1400$) with the attenuated subsample, reduced by the number of missing cases for the wages item, revealed no changes in magnitude beyond .06 for the Pearson r; in fact, most changes were of the order of .03 or less. Comparing the full subsample with the attenuated subsample, reduced by the number of missing cases for the occupation item, revealed no changes in magnitude beyond .04, and most changes were .02 or less.

ly, middle, and late periods of a youth's early career. Table 1 lists these variables by period. Table 2 discloses the exogenous variables.

Table 1
Principal Variable Set of the Study by Period

Early period	Middle period	Late period
first job characteristics	unfavorable job stability	occupational status
tenure on first job	favorable job mobility	wages
low status job reactions	unfavorable job mobility	
aspirations	commitment to work ethic	
motivation		
job-motivation interaction		
job satisfaction		

Table 2
Exogenous Variables of the Study

Demographic	Education	Labor Market
sex	intelligence	urbanization
race	schooling	community size
age		region of residence
socioeconomic status		unemployment rate
marital status		

Principal Variables of the Core Model

A core model establishing relationships between the principal variables of the study is specified and will be elaborated upon in a subsequent section. The purpose of this section is to define the principal variables used in the study. Interested readers are also referred to Appendix B for a fuller description of the variables, including frequencies and selected univariate statistics.

Composite Indices

Before looking at the variables directly, a methodological digression is in order to discuss the construction of indices for variables which were not confined to single indicators. In such cases, composite indices were created on the basis of factor-score coefficients produced as solutions to principal factor analysis.[5] Since many of the components of various composite indices contained nonstandard measures, components were normalized for additive purposes using z-scores. This procedure simply calls for subtracting the mean of a variable from its raw scores and dividing the result by its standard deviation, producing a score which has an effective mean of 0 and a standard deviation of 1. In order to work with positive numbers, a further transformation was executed, multiplying the standard scores by 10 and then adding 50.

Composite indices are constructed at the expense of the independent information provided by the components. Nevertheless, they are used in this research to allow for some parsimony in the model which otherwise would expand to unintelligible proportions. Further, the factor analytic techniques assure reasonable unidimensionality in the constructs.

Other transformations of the data are explained in the text to follow, which discusses the principal variables of the study arranged by period.

---

5. This form of factor analysis differs from principal component analysis in that although factors or composites represent linear combinations of variables, their explanation of an observed variable is both shared and unshared by other variables in its set. In most cases in this study, the solution was further analyzed using orthogonal rotation and, in particular, the varimax criterion. Since the factor matrices resulting from these procedures contain orthogonal factors, the factor coefficients represent both regression weights and correlation coefficients. These coefficients can serve as weights for combination purposes, although in this study factor loadings were sufficiently high and common to employ unweighted factor indices.

Early Period

1. First job characteristics

There are numerous ways to define job characteristics, including psychological, sociological, and economic indicators. The psychological properties were not utilized here since they would have been collinear with a number of response dimensions which subsequently enter the model. Therefore, indicators of first job characteristics chosen initially were the socioeconomic dimensions of occupational status, wages, and hours. Occupational status was measured by the familiar Duncan (1961) Index. This index is ordinal, runs from 3 to 96, and is based on the educational requirements and economic rewards of an occupation. It is oftentimes referred to as a prestige ranking. Wages and hours, the other dimensions considered in the construction of the job characteristics variable, are both interval scale measures, wages representing income from wages and salary in the past year, hours representing the usual hours worked at the current job.

The ultimate choice in the composition of the index for first job characteristics was simply to take the unweighted summation of the occupational status and wages variables. The hours dimension was expressly left out on the basis of a factor analysis revealing two underlying factors in the data. The reason for this configuration seems to be that respondents holding low-level jobs, although working longer hours, still earned less money than those in higher-level jobs. However, for most respondents, longer hours leads to higher wages—a relationship revealed in the second factor. The first factor confirmed the established communality between occupational status and wages, both of which loaded at a coefficient of about .60. As a result, the first factor became the basis for the unweighted composite index for first job characteristics.

2. Tenure on first job

It might be contended that, as an apparent job trait, tenure should be incorporated into the variable of first job characteristics. However, there is disagreement in the literature as to whether tenure is in fact a job characteristic. Although Andrisani uses it this way (Andrisani et al. 1977), others, such as Gibson and Klein (1970), refer to it as an individualistic property. This debate aside, tenure has been shown in the literature to behave in ways sufficiently distinct from job content factors, particularly with respect to subsequent attitudes and experience, to deserve separate treatment here.

The measurement of tenure was straightforward except that a simple divisional computational adjustment was necessitated since the female measure was taken in months whereas the male counterpart was taken in years, the latter considered to be sufficiently sensitive. In addition, recalling the earlier discussion on the subsample, respondents in the original data set having more than seven years of tenure on the job were excluded.

3. Low status job reactions

The remaining variables in the early period constitute career attitudes associated with first job experiences. As explained in chapter 2 in the discussion of the dual labor market (Doeringer and Piore 1971), it is conceivable that holders of low status, secondary jobs develop attitudes which carry over to later employment experience. The low status job reactions variable was created as a dummy variable from an item asked of both the young men and young women. It was asked as follows: "What was the first factor you disliked most about your current job?" Respondents' answers were coded into 25 separate categories. The low-status dummy was created by including response categories characteristic of secondary jobs; i.e., unsatisfactory wages, working conditions, supervision, advancement opportunity, security, steadiness, or importance. The other dummies created from this item included other factors of dissatisfaction and a reference no-answer code.

4. Aspirations

Although the NLS data set does not contain information on pre-employment expectations, it is rich in data regarding various career aspirations once on the job, the latter having been shown to have considerable effects on later employment (Andrisani et al. 1977). To better gauge aspirations, and in particular to control for positive correlations among the various aspiration attributes which could be candidates for composite indexing, difference scores were created. These scores simply took the difference between the aspiration attribute—such as occupation or rate of pay desired—and the current condition. One of the aspiration measures, however, was left in its original form. It asked respondents what they felt their chances were of obtaining the occupation desired at age 30 (age 35 for the young women).

In order to seek unidimensionality in the aspiration variables, a factor analysis was performed. Two of the variables loaded on the first factor which was interpretable. They included: the difference between the occupation of the job the respondent would seek if s/he lost the current job and the occupation of the current job, and the difference between the occupation desired at age 30 and the occupation of the current job. As can be deduced from their construction, these variables are not necessarily theoretically identical. In fact, the former combines aspiration with an element of reality-testing which indeed may thwart aspiration. As it turned out, these variables were negatively correlated. Therefore, a decision was made to use only one indicator of aspirations—the latter, which computes the difference between the occupation desired at age 30 and the occupation of the current job.

5. Motivation

The motivation variable was employed to provide an application of Herzberg's motivation/hygiene theory (Herzberg, Mausner, and Snyderman 1959) incorporating the concepts of job intrinsic and extrinsic factors. The variable was created as a simple recoding of an original variable asking respondents for the first factor they liked most about their current job. The recoding, suggested by the grouping of the original responses, classified the answers into intrinsic or extrinsic categories.

6. Job-motivation interaction

The job-motivation interaction variable was created to provide a direct test of the need-strength theory of job satisfaction (Hackman and Lawler 1971) which suggests that job satisfaction, and by inference, later employment experience, may result from a matching between the individual's job motivation and the nature of the actual job. The interaction variable was constructed as an unweighted multiplicative function of the first job characteristics variable, described earlier, and a different intrinsic-extrinsic motivation variable from the one above. The use of a different motivation variable was considered in order to reduce the chance of multicollinearity. The motivation component was represented by a questionnaire item asking respondents what the most important thing is about their job—liking it or good wages. The former response became the intrinsic factor, the latter the extrinsic factor.

7. Job satisfaction

As is characteristic of most of the work attitudinal measures used in the NLS, job satisfaction was measured by use of a single indicator asking respondents what their attitude was towards their current job. Answers were forced onto a four-point ordinal scale and, for the subsample of this study, are highly weighted towards favorable responses.

The use of a single indicator of overall job satisfaction has come under increasing attack in recent years not only because of the general methodological problem suggesting that the reliability of such an index places an upper bound on its predictive validity (Nunnally 1967), but because there is some question whether it is in fact a valid representation of the complex array of facets it supposedly incorporates (Van Maanen and Katz 1976). Robert Kahn (1972) has suggested that the direct question of satisfaction strikes too closely to one's self-esteem to be answered in an interpretable way.

Nevertheless, Aldag and Brief (1978) have shown that there is as much justification for considering overall job satisfaction to be a linear function of weighted facet scores as a function of alternative nonlinear models. Further, a good deal of accomplished work with the NLS (see, for example, Kohen and Parnes 1971; Kohen and Andrisani 1973; and Kohen et al. 1977) has revealed strong relationships between attitudes and aspects of work experience using the single indicator approach.

Middle Period

The middle period is essentially composed of three variables: job satisfaction 1971, change in employer 1966-1971, and commitment to the work ethic. The first two have been combined into a series of mobility dummy variables. The reason for their inclusion in the core model is provided by evidence from the Career Thresholds studies that mobility under certain conditions can lead to greater advancement in subsequent occupation status (see, for example, Kohen et al. 1977: 98-113). One of the conditions, for example, is the constraining effect of a young person's starting occupational level. Andrisani et al. (1977) further display some evidence that those youth who were dissatisfied with their early job and who subsequently changed employers—with the exception of white males—advanced substantially more in occupational status than their satisfied counterparts. It is appropriate, therefore, to control for the effects of both subsequent change in employer and job satisfaction in establishing relationships between first job experiences and attitudes and later work experience.

The mobility-satisfaction index was constituted, then, of two components. The change in employer variable was dichotomized into two categories: same employer or different employer from first job. The job satisfaction variable was identical to the one used in the early period except that it was taken in 1971 and was recoded into two categories: those who were highly satisfied with their current job, and all others (note that this takes into consideration the aforementioned heavy weighting of positive scores). Dummy variables were then created as follows: (1) those who stayed with the same employer but who were dissatisfied; (2) those who changed employers and were satisfied; and (3) those who changed employers and were dissatisfied. The reference group incorporated those who stayed with the same employer and were satisfied. The principal intent of the dummy variables was to control for the suppressor effect they could have on the principal relationships in the core model. For example, a negative first job experience and its effect on later employment could perhaps be reversed by an intermediate, favorable employer change.[6]

6. Although dummy variables have been used as separate intervening variables in the literature (see, e.g., the application of the measure of educational aspirations in Duncan, Featherman and Duncan 1975, or that of curriculum in Grasso and Shea 1979), some methodologists, particularly econometricians, have attacked this usage (see, e.g., Goldberger 1964: 248-250 or Hanushek and Jackson 1977, chapter 7). They suggest that where categorical dependent variables are used, models should be specified that describe

Besides the mobility-satisfaction index, the middle period contains a generalized commitment variable which is an unweighted composite of two 1971 internal-external locus of control measures, one specific, the other an overall measure. These measures reflect variation among individuals in the payoffs they attribute to initiative (Rotter 1966). They are considered here because they are expected to reflect commitment to the Protestant work ethic. Therefore, in the context of the core model discussed in chapter 1, these measures conceivably are affected by initial job experiences and may, subsequently, have a significant bearing on later employment.

A composite index for commitment to the work ethic was chosen since one of the questions in the Rotter scale of internal-external locus of control asks specifically whether success is a matter of hard work or being at the right place at the right time. An unweighted summation of this measure along with the overall measure effectively gives the specific score the same weight as the overall score. This was confirmed by a factor analysis on the two variables which revealed nearly identical loadings.

Late Period

The late period is made up of two variables, both assessed in 1975: occupational status, represented by the Duncan In-

---

the probabilities of discrete events, or at least in the case of dummy variables, that all categories should be used at once. Canonical correlation can be considered in the latter case (see, e.g., Anderson 1958, chapter 12 or Van der Geer 1971, chapter 14). The efficiency of the estimates of categorical dependent variables can also be improved by applying simultaneous estimation procedures such as two-stage or three-stage least squares (J. Johnston 1972; Malinvaud 1978). Nevertheless, given the broad thrust of this research and the uncertainty about whether in secondary data analysis the more elaborate and cumbersome econometric techniques can truly improve specification, this study has applied the more traditional ordinary least squares approach. The degree of deviation is not expected to be large enough to alter the broad findings for public policy purposes. Further, the least squares procedures, even in equations involving dummy variables, are known to yield consistent estimates according to standard linear assumptions.

dex, and income from wages and salary. Although the choice was made to look at respondents in terms of their final achievement in the labor market at the latest date for which there were data available, the change in status and wages was also deemed important. Therefore, the analysis, as will be discussed in the next section, although predominantly concerned with overall subsequent status, did take into consideration at various points the advancement in status and earnings.

Demographic Variables

This and the next two sections describe the exogenous variables brought into the analysis subsequent to initial development of the core model. They essentially constitute controls on the principal relationships of the model.

The demographic variables include sex, race, age, socioeconomic status, and marital status. The sex variable was made available, as was indicated earlier, by creating male and female subfiles on the basis of a consolidation of the NLS young men and young women cohort data. Race separates the data into white and black respondents. It should be noted that in order to produce statistically reliable estimates for blacks, the NLS oversampled blacks by a ratio of 3 to 1. A small proportion of each of the cohorts also represents other minorities. However, since there were too few to permit any kind of distinct analyses, only data for the white and black respondents were included in this study.

Age was specified by the sampling requirements of the NLS youth cohorts which initially surveyed individuals between the ages of 14 and 24. Socioeconomic status was based on the Duncan Index of parent's occupation. Since the Duncan Index incorporates educational and income dimensions in its construction, it is commonly considered to be an index of social class.[7] The parent's occupation was construed as father's occupation unless such data were unavailable. In that instance, an assumption was made that the mother might be working as a single head of household. Therefore, mother's occupation was used when father's occupation was missing.

Finally, marital status was converted to three dummy variables: married; divorced, separated, or widowed; and single. The original spouse absent category was used as the reference group.

Education Variables

The education variables included two measures, intelligence and schooling, both of which are composites. The intelligence variable represents the unweighted summation of two measures: the IQ score with values running from 40 to 160 and the Knowledge of World of Work total score, the values of which were standardized to account for the difference in scaling for men and women. The IQ component represents an aptitude measure, whereas the Knowledge of World of Work component represents an achievement measure corresponding to familiarity with aspects of particular trades and professions. Both components loaded nearly identically on one factor in a separate factor analysis, justifying their summation.

The schooling composite was made up of years of formal education, measured by the highest grade completed as of the first date for which data were available (1966 for men, 1968 for women) and a training variable, measured by a yes-no response to a question asking respondents whether they took occupational training programs in the past year (asked

7. For an excellent review of evidence associating the Duncan Index with socioeconomic status, see Hauser and Featherman (1977: 3-8).

in 1967 for the men, 1969 for the women). Again, justification for their summation was provided by a separate factor analysis.

Labor Market Variables

The labor market variables included four measures: urbanization, community size, region of residence, and unemployment rate. Urbanization, measured by current residence in a SMSA, was transformed into two dummy variables: living in the SMSA in the central city and living in the SMSA but not in the central city, i.e., a suburb. The response—not in the SMSA—was used as the reference category.

Community size was represented by an ordinal variable based on a scale of 1 to 8 in order of decreasing size of residence according to 1960 Census figures. The scale runs from urbanized areas of 3 million or more population to rural areas of under 2,500 population.

Region of residence was measured by the nine Census divisions of residence of the United States proper. Categories were dummied, leaving the last or ninth division, the Pacific, as the reference category.

Finally, unemployment rate represented the actual unemployment rate, in the case of the men recorded in 1967 for the labor market of the 1966 residence, and in the case of the women recorded in 1968 for the labor market of the 1968 residence. Although there is an effective difference of one year in the computation of the unemployment measure between the men and the women, the variation is not expected to be significant. In fact, a scan of unemployment rates in 150 major labor areas between the years 1967 and 1968 revealed only five areas where the fluctuation was greater than 1 percent (Manpower Report of the President, 1974). In general, there was minimal unemployment fluctuation between these years of the high economic growth period of the late Sixties.

Analysis

Methodological Framework

The analytic framework of this study incorporates a number of methods, all of which are directed towards the specification of a theoretical model of initial job experiences and later employment. The rudiments of such a model should contain, according to Homans (1966), a set of interrelated propositions which identify and establish an order among the relevant properties leading to a deductive system. As a basis of theoretical development, the model will depend upon prior conceptual and empirical analysis but hopefully will also serve as a springboard for further specification and estimation.

At the outset the author is suggesting that theory has not been sufficiently developed in this area to work solely on estimation, which would involve fitting data to a specified model. Certainly, as the review of the literature would imply, there is an abundance of both theoretical and empirical studies of a variety of questions having to do with initial job experiences and attitudes of youth in their early careers. However, this literature tends to focus on isolated variables from particular disciplines rather than on the interrelated system proposed here, oftentimes is cross-sectional and deals with restrictive samples, and as a result does not contain the necessary features to make comparisons to other contexts or to have general applicability across time. Further, although the literature has advanced markedly in its empirical sophistication, there still is some reliance on zero-order relationships which contain strong *ceteris paribus* assumptions. We need to move, consequently, to model specification which can begin to unfold the complex causal structure of career and labor market experiences and attitudes.

In this study, although a causal model is not entirely specified, an attempt is made to introduce the key properties and interactions which form the basis for such a model. The reason for taking this approach is that, in the opinion of the author, it is still premature to specify a model and then resort to the empiricist position of "letting the data speak for themselves" (Goldberger 1968: chap. 9). Rather, it seems more appropriate at this time to develop a model through the intermittent application of theory and data analysis. In this way, the model may be shaped or in Heise's (1969) words "trimmed" so that it can be more completely specified. The approach is therefore exploratory in that it represents an initial step to calibrate the model with real data.

More precisely, the analytic framework adopted here employs in various forms three approaches common to social research: the block-recursive design, the Simon-Blalock technique, and path analysis. The longitudinal periods defined previously—early, middle, and late—essentially constitute blocks of indicators which are hypothesized to be causally related (Sullivan 1971). The early period contains three blocks, the middle period two blocks, and the late period one block. However, no assumption is made about the causal interrelations of the indicators in any one block of indicators. They may be causally related to one another apart from the spuriousness produced by the assumption that the indicators are at least partially caused by the underlying factor. Even if unrelated to one another, the important point is that by assuming a block recursive design, we focus on relationships between but not within blocks. This involves using the indicators of the dependent variable separately, and allowing the indicators of the independent and control variables to operate as a block. In this way, theory essentially guides our selection of the best indicators of a given construct as opposed to strict empirical reductive techniques.

The Simon-Blalock technique (Simon 1957; Blalock 1964) uses similar logic. It overidentifies a structural model on the basis of the theory; that is, it deletes one or more paths from a so-called "just determined model" in which all possible recursive paths are included. In this way, the overidentified model allows the researcher the necessary information to test the model's goodness of fit to the observed data (Griffin 1977).

The Simon-Blalock technique, although a form of structural modeling, is considered by some (see, for example, Boudon 1965; Heise 1969; and Duncan 1975) to be weak and restricted compared to path analysis. The latter approach offers a more powerful test of structural relationships. Unlike the Simon-Blalock technique which tests the significance of only the hypothesized zero paths, path analysis tests the significance of all paths. Then, those paths which are by some criterion considered trivial or nonsignificant may be deleted. The "trimmed" model may then be estimated (Heise 1969).

In this study a core model is represented by hypothesizing recursive paths between six blocks of variables, as is illustrated in Figure 1. The first block contains the early job characteristics variables; the second, the early career attitude variables; the third, the job satisfaction measure; the fourth, the job mobility-satisfaction dummies; the fifth, the commitment variable; and the sixth, the later work experience criterion measures. No causal links are established within the blocks, according to theoretical judgment—a position favored by the Simon-Blalock technique. However, corresponding to the path analytic approach, the core model is respecified by trimming on all the available paths. This

Figure 1
Core Model Using Block Recursive Design

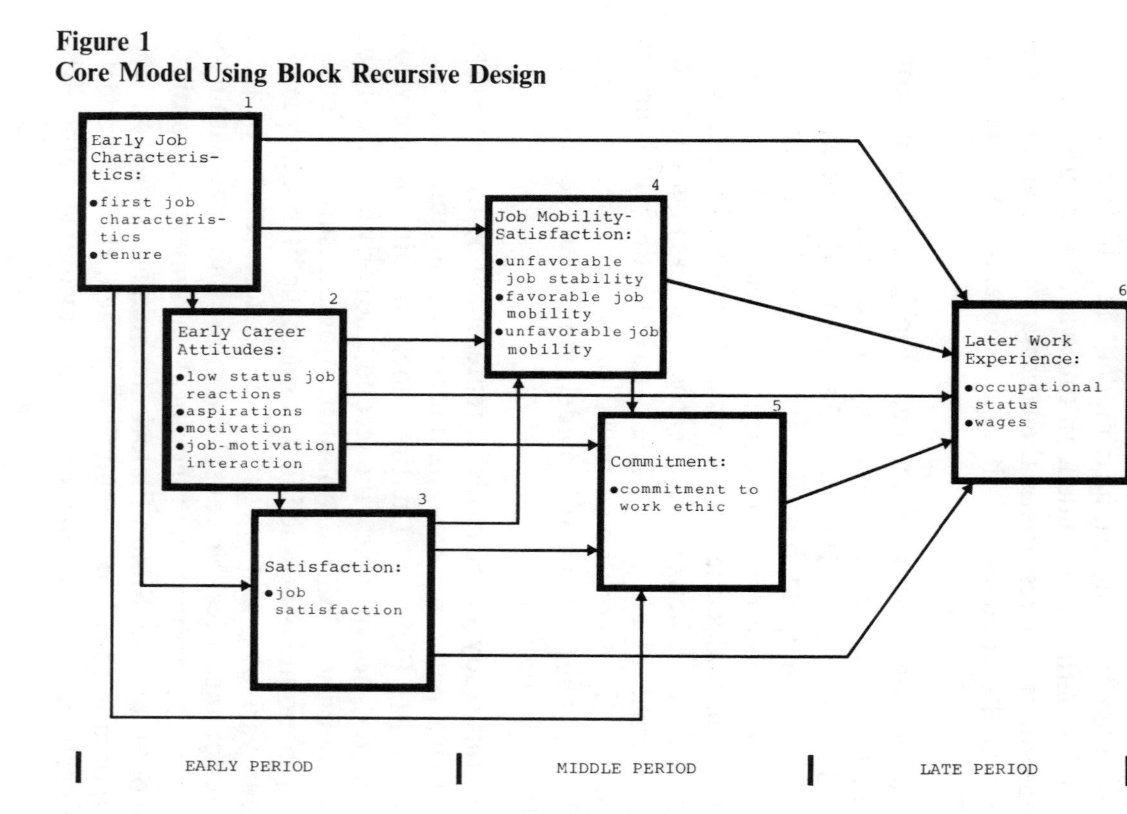

specification is provisional as it can be further adjusted and then estimated by researchers employing different data sets. However, the trimmed core model is issued here hopefully as a substantial advancement on a theory of initial job experiences and later employment.

Model Testing

The basis for trimming the core model and then testing its parameters was the same; the criterion used was the ordinary least squares estimation procedure (Blalock 1964). According to this procedure, the following model is applied:

$$Y' = A + B_1X_1 + B_2X_2 + \ . \ . \ . \ + B_kX_k$$

where Y' represents the estimated value for Y, the dependent variable; A is the Y intercept; and the B_i are regression coefficients. The A and B_i coefficients are selected in such a way that the sum of squared residuals $\Sigma\ (Y\text{-}Y')^2$ is minimized. In path analysis, the estimation of the path or partial regression coefficients simply requires a series of regressions, taking one variable at a time—in this case, a block of variables—as the dependent variable and all the variables with higher causal order as the independent variables. It is necessary initially before trimming to solve (n-1) regression equations if the model contains n variables.[8]

All regressions performed as tests of the core model as well as the other computational and statistical techniques used in this study were run on the SPSS computer package (Nie et al. 1975).

8. According to standard path analytic procedure, it is suggested that when estimating overidentified models a goodness-of-fit test be used which assesses the ability of the estimated model to reproduce the observed data (correlations). This involves computing a reproduced correlation matrix based on parameter estimates and a X^2 test of the significance of the difference between the observed and reproduced correlation matrix (see Joreskog 1967; Burt 1973). Such a test was not indicated for this study, however, given its block recursive nature which represents overidentification only to the extent of paths within blocks which are purposely excluded. The remaining paths are just determined.

Other features of the application of the core model should also be noted. First, due to the unavoidable situation of having to work with missing values caused by attrition in the longitudinal data, regressions were computed on the basis of a "pairwise present" correlation matrix. In such a matrix each correlation coefficient is based on the subset of respondents for which neither of any required pair of variables has a missing value.

Second, for reporting purposes, standardized regression coefficients were used rather than unstandardized coefficients. The reason for this choice was that since the independent variables were expected in almost every case to be measured in different units, the standardized coefficients would provide a sensible way to compare the relative effect on the dependent variable of each independent variable. Furthermore, the effects are reported for the NLS population alone. On the other hand, it should be pointed out for the benefit of subsequent researchers that the establishment of causal laws may be better served by using unstandardized coefficients (see, for example, Blalock 1967; Schoenberg 1972; and Duncan 1975).

Although the standardized coefficients were reported, the criterion used to test the triviality or nonsignificance of the model paths was that of statistical significance which incorporates the unstandardized coefficient. One familiar test, adopted here, simply requires that this coefficient be twice its standard error, which at large enough degrees of freedom should guarantee significance at the minimum .05 level. This is because the t statistic, which is produced by this formulation, at degrees of freedom of 60 or more, is significant at this level. It should be noted that SPSS computes F ratios as tests of significance of the individual regression coefficients entered in standard nonhierarchical form. These F's are readily interpretable, however, since their square root furnishes the t statistic.

Subgroup Analysis

It should be recognized that the core model, which essentially represents an average of career patterns of the youth population, shields persistent patterns typical of important subgroups of that population. Therefore, it is necessary to view the career patterns of these subgroups in terms of how they each perform when analyzed according to the core model. The following subgroups were considered:

- male - female
- white - black
- less than high school education - high school education - college education +
- low, middle, high socioeconomic status
- disadvantaged - nondisadvantaged
- 14-17 - 18-20 - 21-24 years of age
- urban - suburban - rural
- low, middle, high job level
- less than one year of tenure - more than one year of tenure

Some subgroup interactions were also examined. The analysis focused on how each separate subgroup varied from the overall core model.

Each subgroup, as can be seen above, is made up of separate categories which together form a variable. Therefore, in order to examine between-group variation on the respective dependent variables of the core model, the means of each of the categories for each subgroup were inspected using oneway analysis of variance and, where there were at least three nonempty categories, were further tested using an *a posteriori* contrast or range test (Winer 1971). According to these tests, such as the Student-Neuman-Keuls procedure, the difference between all possible pairs of group means divided into homogeneous subsets is tested for significance, for example, at the .05 level. SNK, which was used in this study, considers different range values for different size subsets.[9]

Following the examination of the subgroups, the analysis concluded by entering the demographic, education, and labor market variables (see Table 2), many of which were separately inspected in the subgroup analysis, into the trimmed core model. This final procedure would disclose the linear effects of these exogenous variables on the core model thus incorporating into the theory of initial job experiences and later employment the role of environmental preconditions.

---

9. There are formal tests to ascertain whether subgroups of a population should be included in an overall model through the use of dummy variables or whether the model should be estimated separately by stratifying the observations into separate data sets (see, e.g., Chow 1960). Since all subgroups are uniformly analyzed in this study, it is conceivable that some of them may not interact with variables in the model. They are nevertheless presented for interest so that the reader can observe the behavior of the core model for these exogenous groups. Since the core model gives a *ceteris paribus* estimate, policymakers in particular should have the opportunity to observe its effects for targeted subgroups. Finally, on the basis of what we already know from theory and practice, the separate analyses and interpretations of these particular subgroups are likely to be accurate in thrust.

Chapter 4
Results

The results are reported first on the basis of the analysis of the core model for the overall sample. Then, the various subgroup analyses are considered in order to demonstrate the varying patterns of the core model revealed by different demographic groups as well as to explore some bivariate effects. The last section of results discloses the expanded, full model which incorporates the exogenous demographic, education, and labor market variables into the trimmed core model.

Readers might wish to focus only on those subgroup analyses which are of interest to them.[1] Moreover, those interested strictly in an overview of the findings or who wish to avoid the technical detail in the separate analyses could skip immediately to the next chapter for the summary.

Overall Sample

The results of the core model analysis are displayed in tabular form in Table 3. Figure 2 depicts these results in a

1. Readers are also alerted to the fact that some of the subgroup analyses suffer from dangerously low degrees of freedom. These cases are pointed out in the text. In order to uphold the standards of statistical significance used in calibrating the model, the magnitude of significant relationships to be reported according to the F ratio is naturally reduced. However, interpretations are offered for the relationships revealed on the basis of previously reported theory, the author's knowledge of patterns in the data, and the assumption that the subgroup data sets are sufficient in reflecting their larger populations.

Table 3
Path Regression Results of the Analysis of the Core Model for the Overall Sample

Significant paths	BETA	F	DF	R	R^2
Occupational status 1975			11 412	.6594	.4348
Unfavorable job stability	-.1074	4.697			
Unfavorable job mobility	-.1126	4.914			
Aspirations	.1977	22.958			
First job characteristics	.6229	158.624			
Wages 1975			11 412	.3786	.1433
Commitment to work ethic	-.1674	12.770			
Favorable job mobility	-.1274	4.465			
Unfavorable job mobility	-.1608	6.609			
First job characteristics	.2942	23.352			
Tenure on first job	.1282	7.366			
Commitment to work ethic			10 413	.2303	.0530
None					
Unfavorable job stability			7 416	.2332	.0544
Job-motivation interaction	-.1223	4.392			
Tenure on first job	.1691	12.254			
Favorable job mobility			7 416	.1447	.0209
Tenure on first job	-.1097	4.985			
Unfavorable job mobility			7 416	.2598	.0675
First job characteristics	-.2094	11.428			
Tenure on first job	-.1193	6.194			
Job satisfaction			6 678	.3540	.1253
Job-motivation interaction	.1037	5.611			
Motivation	.1140	9.967			
Aspirations	-.1972	25.418			
Low status job reactions	-.1592	19.408			
Low status job reactions			2 1191	.0463	.0021
None					
Aspirations			2 682	.3713	.1379
First job characteristics	-.3714	106.763			

Table 3 (continued)

Significant paths	BETA	F	DF	R	R^2
Motivation			2 1178	.0236	.0005
None					
Job-motivation interaction			1 1199	.0388	.0015
None					

Key to path regression tables

Only paths significant at the .05 level according to the *F* ratio with N-k-1 degrees of freedom are reported.

BETA column lists the standardized partial-regression coefficients.

F column represents the *F* ratio for each individual independent variable with 1 and N-k-1 degrees of freedom.

DF are the degrees of freedom for the entire regression run including all paths. Therefore, they contain k independent variables in the equation with degrees of freedom N-k-1.

R is the multiple correlation coefficient for the entire equation.

R^2 is the coefficient of determination or the ratio of the amount of variance in the dependent variable explained by the independent variables in the equation.

Figure 2
Analysis of the Core Model for the Overall Sample

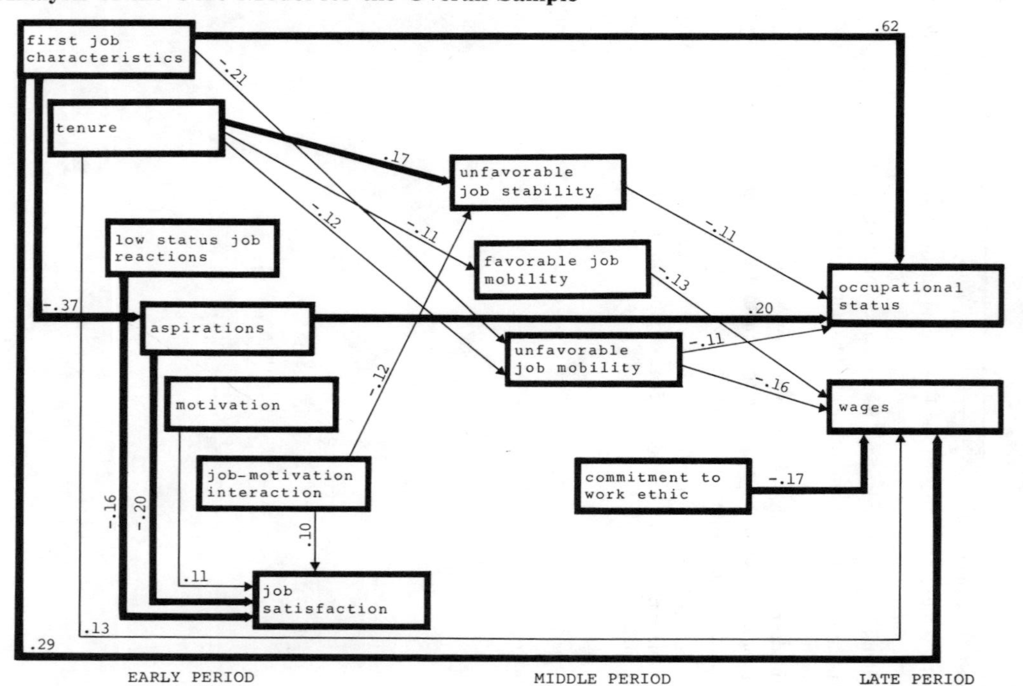

All paths indicated are significant beyond the .05 level according to the *F* ratio with N-k-1 degrees of freedom. Bold line paths are significant at .001. Path coefficients are standardized regression coefficients.

path diagram. Discussion of the findings will proceed by reviewing independent effects of the early period variables on the principal dependent variables: occupational status and wages in 1975; independent effects of the middle period variables; and finally indirect effects and other intermediate paths of interest. Conclusions reached should be considered as effects on a youth's early career due to work experience and attitudinal factors. These conclusions, however, are tempered by the exogenous effects to be manifested in the ensuing sections.

Early Period Effects

With respect to early period effects on the dependent variables, the overall results confirm a commonly accepted finding of the literature that the first job has a significant bearing on later work experience. For both occupational status and wages, it is apparent that first job characteristics accounts for most of the variance explained. It is also important to point out that whereas the beta coefficient is strong and positive (.62) in explaining later occupational status, it is reasonably strong but negative (-.31) if the regression is run on *change* in later occupational status as the dependent variable. Therefore, although it pays to have a good initial job, hope is held out for some youngsters who start low. Regardless of whether the absolute or change occupational status variable is used, aspirations accounts for a good portion of the variance and, confirming the findings of Andrisani et al. (1977), is positively related to later occupational status. It is the only early career attitude associated with later work experience, job satisfaction being notably absent. Finally, tenure on the first job is found to be significantly related to later wages, denoting perhaps the financial benefits accruing from job stability or from adjustment to the job environment (Hulin and Smith 1965).

Middle Period Effects

The middle period variables are active in the core model analysis, particularly the job mobility-satisfaction variables. The presence of different pairs of these dummies in the paths to the separate dependent variables suggests that one of the components is stronger in each case. For occupational status, since the paths are from the first and third dummies, the focus is on the attitudes generated in this period, since regardless of job mobility, unfavorable dispositions towards one's job affects ultimate status. In the case of wages, it appears that job mobility has negatively affected later wages regardless of whether the respondent has expressed satisfaction or dissatisfaction with his/her job. However, dissatisfaction along with job mobility has a most serious effect on later wages and occupational status. These conclusions were borne out by examining zero-order correlations of the separate components of the job mobility-satisfaction index.

The other middle period effect to be reported here is disconcerting, but perhaps premature given that the results are for the overall sample. Commitment to the work ethic is not only not observed as intervening between early job experiences and attitudes and later employment, but is negatively related to later wages. The strong negative coefficient persists when change in wages is used in place of absolute wages. This finding is directly contradictory to those of Andrisani et al. (1977), although their study did not include young women and represented both an earlier and shorter span of time between the observed relationships. The subsequent subgroup analyses might be revealing as regards this particular finding.

Other Effects

Figure 2 demonstrates quite clearly the intervening nature of the job mobility-satisfaction variables between early job experiences and attitudes and later employment. Tenure on first job is significantly related to each of the dummies. The sign changes indicate that tenure is positively related to job dissatisfaction when the first job is retained into the middle period. Tenure is also negatively related to job mobility regardless of satisfaction. Further, from the previous section we know that job mobility has a deleterious effect on later wages and, in combination with dissatisfaction, on later status as well. Therefore, for the overall sample, there are benefits to be gained financially by staying with one's first job, especially if one has had tenure on that job originally. As revealed by the first dummy, this conclusion must be conditioned by job attitudes, since dissatisfaction in the middle period on the retained job can be costly in terms of occupational status.

Unfavorable job mobility is also intervening between first job characteristics and later work experience, indicating that a low-level unstable first job may lead to job mobility and dissatisfaction, both of which in the middle period are negative precursors of later employment.

Aspirations is also intervening between first job characteristics and later occupational status. The negative sign of the first path in this set of relationships reveals the power that aspirations can have in reversing a potentially negative effect on later employment forecast by a low-level job. Apparently, for some youth, high occupational aspirations can overcome initial barriers to later career success.

The role of early occupational aspirations is further developed by viewing their effects on initial job satisfaction. The negative relationship between aspirations and job satisfaction suggests that the affirmative role that aspirations play in later work experience perhaps stems from the fact that youngsters with high aspirations don't like their first job.

Besides aspirations, all the other early career attitudes are associated with job satisfaction. Low status job reactions are, as expected, negatively related to job satisfaction. Intrinsic motivation is positively associated with job satisfaction, confirming the theory of Herzberg, Mausner, and Snyderman (1959). Also, lending support to need-strength theorists (Hackman and Lawler 1971; Brief and Aldag 1975), interaction between the job and individual needs accounts for some of the variance in job satisfaction, apart from the separate contributions of intrinsic motivation and the job itself. It is interesting to note, moreover, that although intrinsic motivation is in the equation, first job characteristics is not. The latter re-emerges, however, when the interaction variable is left out of the equation. Although this may be a statistical artifact produced by using the first job characteristics variable as a component of the interaction variable, it may also indicate that job-motivation interaction has separate and perhaps more significant explanatory power than the job alone in accounting for job attitudes.

Finally, although job satisfaction is a wealthy recipient of paths, for the overall sample at any rate, it has no future career effects. This finding has to be reviewed more carefully in the subgroup analyses to follow since as it now stands, limited support is rendered, from a career point of view, for continuing job satisfaction research.

Overall Sample - Trimmed

According to the methodology discussed in chapter 3, the core model can be respecified by resubmitting the data to regression analysis, but this time including only significant paths resulting from the initial analysis. This procedure was undertaken for the overall sample.

The results are displayed in Table 4 in the form of a "trimmed" analysis. It is apparent that the findings from the in-

Table 4
Path Regression Results of the Trimmed Analysis of the Core Model for the Overall Sample

Significant paths	BETA	F	DF	R	R^2
Occupational status 1975			4 419	.6515	.4245
Unfavorable job stability	-.1103	7.563			
Unfavorable job mobility	-.1140	7.740			
Aspirations	.2185	29.831			
First job characteristics	.6657	264.836			
Wages 1975			5 584	.3617	.1308
Commitment to work ethic	-.1645	17.647			
Favorable job mobility	-.0953	5.184			
Unfavorable job mobility	-.1259	8.586			
First job characteristics	.2392	35.308			
Tenure on first job	.1284	10.404			
Unfavorable job stability			2 649	.1965	.0386
Job-motivation interaction	-.0915	5.650			
Tenure on first job	.1775	21.242			
Favorable job mobility			1 686	.1053	.0111
Tenure on first job	-.1053	7.699			
Unfavorable job mobility			2 662	.2442	.0596
First job characteristics	-.1974	26.852			
Tenure on first job	-.1176	9.535			
Job satisfaction			4 730	.3513	.1234
Job-motivation interaction	.1300	13.709			
Motivation	.1127	10.475			
Aspirations	-.2112	35.585			
Low status job reactions	-.1589	20.778			
Aspirations			1 767	.3713	.1379
First job characteristics	-.3713	122.710			

itial analysis need no respecification; in fact, all original paths remain in the second analysis. Further, the variables appearing in the original analysis appear to be sufficiently robust since the trimmed analysis explains almost as much of the variance in each path equation. In fact, R-squares in the restricted analysis are never less than .02 from their counterparts in the original, more inclusive version. Hence, for the variables selected in the core model, representing a theory of initial job experiences and later employment, the analysis for the overall sample is complete.

Subgroup Analysis: Sex

In this section, the core model is analyzed for young males and young females. Differences between these sex categories will be examined as well as differences from the overall sample.

Males

The young male analysis is remarkably similar to the overall analysis and certainly as rich in detail (see Table 5 and Figure 3). Forty-one percent of the variance in later occupational status is explained as compared to 43 percent for the overall sample. A respectable increase in the variance explained for later wages is found for the male subgroup, from 14 to 32 percent. This is accounted for largely by the importance to the young men of first job characteristics. The beta coefficient for this early period variable is .52. Further, compared to the overall sample, tenure on the first job does not appear in the equation for later wages. Other early period effects on wages for the young men are found for aspirations and job satisfaction, the latter being negative. Since aspirations are negatively related to job satisfaction, this augments the preliminary conclusion arrived at in the overall analysis that high aspirations, either apart from or as a result of

Table 5
Path Regression Results of the Analysis of the Core Model for the Subgroup Category: Males

Significant paths	BETA	F	DF	R	R^2
			11		
Occupational status 1975			336	.6417	.4119
Unfavorable job mobility	-.1270	4.506			
Job-motivation interaction	.1027	4.152			
Aspirations	.1771	14.621			
First job characteristics	.5809	114.650			
			11		
Wages 1975			336	.5664	.3209
Unfavorable job stability	-.1770	7.672			
Favorable job mobility	-.1955	10.413			
Unfavorable job mobility	-.2315	12.976			
Job satisfaction	-.1102	4.987			
Aspirations	.1162	5.450			
First job characteristics	.5235	80.638			
			10		
Commitment to work ethic			337	.3481	.1212
Job satisfaction	.1201	4.659			
First job characteristics	.1503	5.233			
Tenure on first job	.1631	9.453			
			7		
Unfavorable job stability			346	.2552	.0651
Job-motivation interaction	-.1393	5.078			
First job characteristics	.1580	5.834			
Tenure on first job	.1590	8.968			
			7		
Favorable job mobility			346	.1337	.0178
None					
			7		
Unfavorable job mobility			346	.2711	.0735
First job characteristics	-.2349	13.020			
Tenure on first job	-.1065	4.061			
			6		
Job satisfaction			505	.3802	.1445
Motivation	.1709	16.878			
Aspirations	-.2256	26.217			
Low status job reactions	-.1519	13.471			

Table 5 (continued)

Significant paths	BETA	F	DF	R	R^2
			2		
Low status job reactions			568	.0413	.0017
None					
			2		
Aspirations			509	.3257	.1061
First job characteristics	-.3214	56.649			
			2		
Motivation			566	.0509	.0026
None					
			1		
Job-motivation interaction			568	.0697	.0048
None					

Figure 3
Analysis of the Core Model for the Subgroup Category: Males

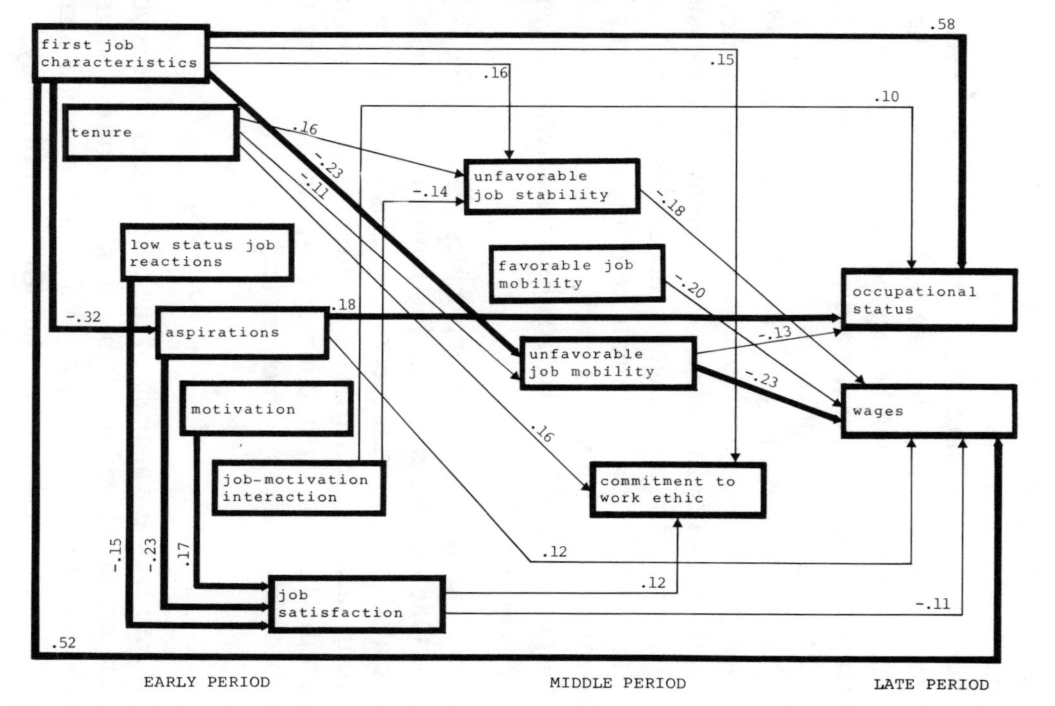

All paths indicated are significant beyond the .05 level according to the *F* ratio with N-k-1 degrees of freedom. Bold line paths are significant at .001. Path coefficients are standardized regression coefficients.

dissatisfaction with the first job, can lead to later financial gain in work.

In the middle period, both job mobility and dissatisfaction, separately or in combination, are found to negatively affect later wages. The job mobility-satisfaction variables are also intervening between some of the early period variables and later work experience. The shorter the tenure, the lower the job level, the more likely the male youngster will be dissatisfied if he changes jobs, and these conditions will negatively affect later work experience. However, if he finds a job which meets his needs, he will tend to keep it, although satisfaction will be dependent on the job's quality and tenure. Finally, reversing a disconcerting finding of the overall sample, commitment to the work ethic, though not statistically significant and therefore not reported, is, however, positively related to later wages. This indicates that the negative relationship observed in the overall analysis between commitment and wages is accounted for by women who, as shall be seen, though committed to work, earn substantially less than men. Finally, for young men, commitment is positively affected by first job characteristics, tenure, and job satisfaction.

Other findings for the young males resemble the overall results. One exception is that job-motivation interaction is not related to job satisfaction, suggesting that for this subgroup category, intrinsic motivation is most important in accounting for job satisfaction apart from the job or from the match between one's motives and one's job.

Females

The results of the analysis of the core model for the young women are displayed in Table 6 and Figure 4 and are astonishing, to say the least. Whereas the men's analysis resembles and perhaps enriches the overall analysis, the

Table 6
Path Regression Results of the Analysis of the Core Model for the Subgroup Category: Females

Significant paths	BETA	F	DF	R	R^2
			11		
Occupational status 1975			58	.6840	.4679
Aspirations	.2809	5.440			
First job characteristics	.7424	26.013			
			11		
Wages 1975			58	.2949	.0869
None					
			10		
Commitment to work ethic			59	.1822	.0332
None					
			7		
Unfavorable job stability			62	.1922	.0369
None					
			7		
Favorable job mobility			62	.1677	.0281
None					
			7		
Unfavorable job mobility			62	.3069	.0941
None					
			6		
Job satisfaction			155	.3195	.1020
Low status job reactions	-.1759	5.258			
			2		
Low status job reactions			603	.0300	.0009
None					
			2		
Aspirations			167	.5543	.3073
First job characteristics	-.5647	73.991			
			2		
Motivation			593	.0513	.0026
None					
			1		
Job-motivation interaction			629	.0903	.0081
Tenure on first job	.0903	5.174			

Figure 4
Analysis of the Core Model for the Subgroup Category: Females

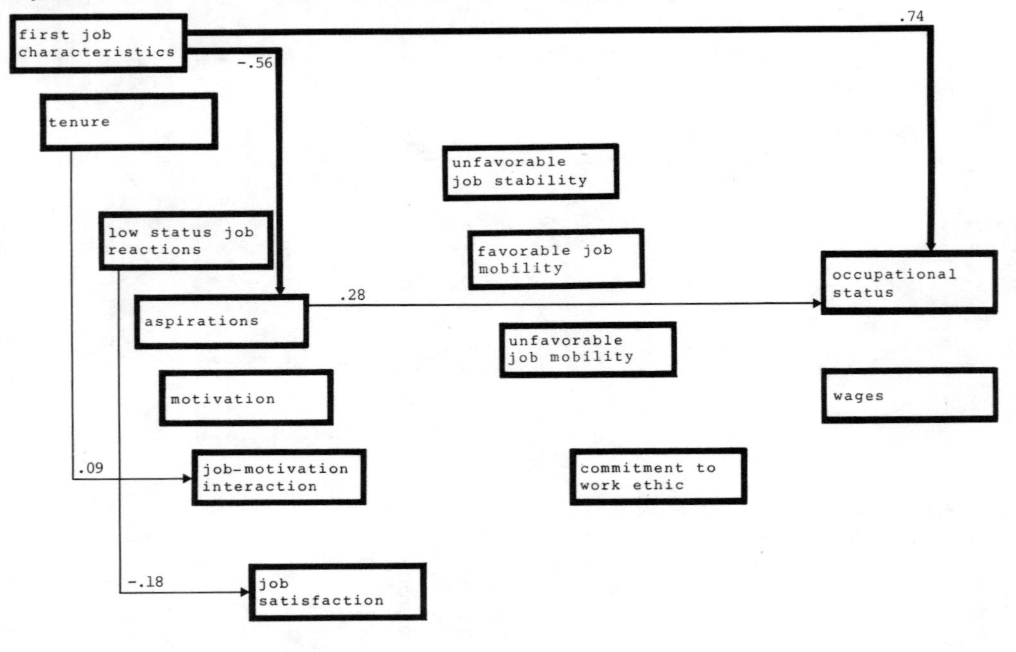

All paths indicated are significant beyond the .05 level according to the *F* ratio with N-k-1 degrees of freedom. Bold line paths are significant at .001. Path coefficients are standardized regression coefficients.

women's analysis is striking in its impoverishment. Its paths do not reveal any new directions; there are simply very few of them to examine. This suggests paying as much attention to the absence of paths as to their presence. It also suggests, on a general theoretical level, that such "status attainment" researchers as Tyree and Treas (1974), Treiman and Terrell (1975), Featherman and Hauser (1976), and McClendon (1976) are right in stipulating that women follow different career routes and eventually reach different labor force destinations from men. Regarding the latter conclusion, in this study it is important at the outset of the discussion of the young women's results to note that although by 1975 the female sample enjoys equivalent occupational status to the men (in fact, a oneway analysis of variance indicates that they do significantly better), they are drastically behind in wages. Mean wages for the women are 3,869 dollars, compared to 10,131 for the men. Further, and this perhaps accounts for the absence of paths to later wages in the women's sample, the standard deviation for the women is 3,775 dollars, compared to 7,472 for the men. As Sorkin (1973) explains, women may have equal prestige to men, but they are concentrated into a narrower range of lower-paying jobs.

Additional *a posteriori* contrast tests on the data for the sex categories reveal that women, contrary to the findings of Brayfield and Wells (1957) and Siegel (1971), are significantly more satisfied with their first job and more committed to the work ethic than men. However, they are less intrinsically motivated and have lower career aspirations.

With respect to the core model analysis, the basic scenario for young women, according to the findings for later occupational status, is that the way to get ahead is to get a good first job or to have high career aspirations, and that the latter may even overcome a bad first job in terms of career growth. However, nothing in the model suggests a way to avoid discrimination, particularly in wages. Even though women start out at lower wages than men, the data for this sample in a separate analysis indicate women's growth in wages since the first job to be under a fifth that of men, although these results are overstated since the young women's span is two years less than that of the young men.

The literature has substantiated these findings. Becker (1957) specified labor market discrimination as a wage differential created by the employer not out of a profit motive but rather as a way to indulge his tastes about the composition of his work force. Bergmann (1971) referred to discrimination as occupational discrimination which crowds women into a limited number of low paying, low productivity jobs. In a comprehensive test of sexual disparities in employment, Almquist (1979) found that discrimination against women was pervasive, costly, and occurred without distinction among subgroups of women due to the fact that employers treat women as a class.

Since the focus of this study is longitudinal, it is interesting to note that the results go beyond the end-points of discrimination. They indicate that discrimination likely occurs as a process throughout a woman's career. Tsuchigane and Dodge (1974) reveal such processual discrimination to be a result of hiring, of social and cultural conditioning, or sex role socialization, all of which inhibit most women's aspirations and prevent them from developing interests in and capabilities for pursuing and succeeding in certain lines of work. For example, Hennig and Jardim (1977) explain that women generally make career decisions relatively late in life and that they see their jobs as a here-and-now means of self-fulfillment rather than as a step in a career progression. The present study indicates that those women who have high career aspirations can advance in occupational status, but not in wages. Now perhaps these findings are largely influenced by the time period in question which, in the early period, precedes both the Women's Movement and equal opportunity legislation. Nevertheless, such public policy changes cannot truly guarantee equal access nor can they ensure that "people who have been traditionally discriminated against will immediately and automatically demonstrate the ability to take advantage of whatever access to opportunity may exist" (Hennig and Jardim 1977: 12).

Secondary findings of the women's analysis are that low status job reactions negatively affect job satisfaction and that tenure is positively related to job-motivation interaction. The latter, being a different finding from either the overall or the men's analyses, appears to indicate that women are more adaptable to jobs over time; i.e., the longer they stay on their first job, the more it will come into line with their needs or vice-versa.

Subgroup Analysis: Race

Whites

Table 7 and Figure 5 reveal that the results of the analyses for the category, whites, constitute essentially a subset of the overall sample results. The only new path is between aspirations and favorable job mobility, which a separate component analysis revealed arises mainly because of the rather substantial negative relationship between aspirations and job satisfaction in the middle period. This seems to indicate that for whites, youth with high aspirations continue to be dissatisfied with either their old or new job in the middle period, presumably because their aspirations have still not been met.

The principal paths noticeably missing are from the job mobility-satisfaction variables to the two dependent variables. Only unfavorable job mobility is related to wages.

Table 7
Path Regression Results of the Analysis of the Core Model for the Subgroup Category: Whites

Significant paths	BETA	F	DF	R	R^2
Occupational status 1975			11 299	.6178	.3816
Aspirations	.1761	11.425			
First job characteristics	.5962	103.397			
Wages 1975			11 299	.3595	.1292
Commitment to work ethic	-.1824	11.044			
Unfavorable job mobility	-.1433	4.128			
First job characteristics	.2696	15.017			
Commitment to work ethic			10 300	.1836	.0337
None					
Unfavorable job stability			7 303	.2242	.0502
Tenure on first job	.1643	8.370			
Favorable job mobility			7 303	.1861	.0346
Aspirations	-.1336	4.387			
Tenure on first job	-.1196	4.364			
Unfavorable job mobility			7 303	.2830	.0801
First job characteristics	-.2401	11.926			
Tenure on first job	-.1187	4.510			
Job satisfaction			6 488	.3327	.1107
Job-motivation interaction	.1016	4.078			
Motivation	.1144	7.030			
Aspirations	-.1928	16.505			
Low status job reactions	-.1441	11.122			
Low status job reactions			2 860	.0524	.0027
None					
Aspirations			2 492	.3989	.1591
First job characteristics	-.3886	86.771			
Motivation			2 870	.0309	.0009
None					
Job-motivation interaction			1 865	.0079	.0000
None					

Figure 5
Analysis of the Core Model for the Subgroup Category: Whites

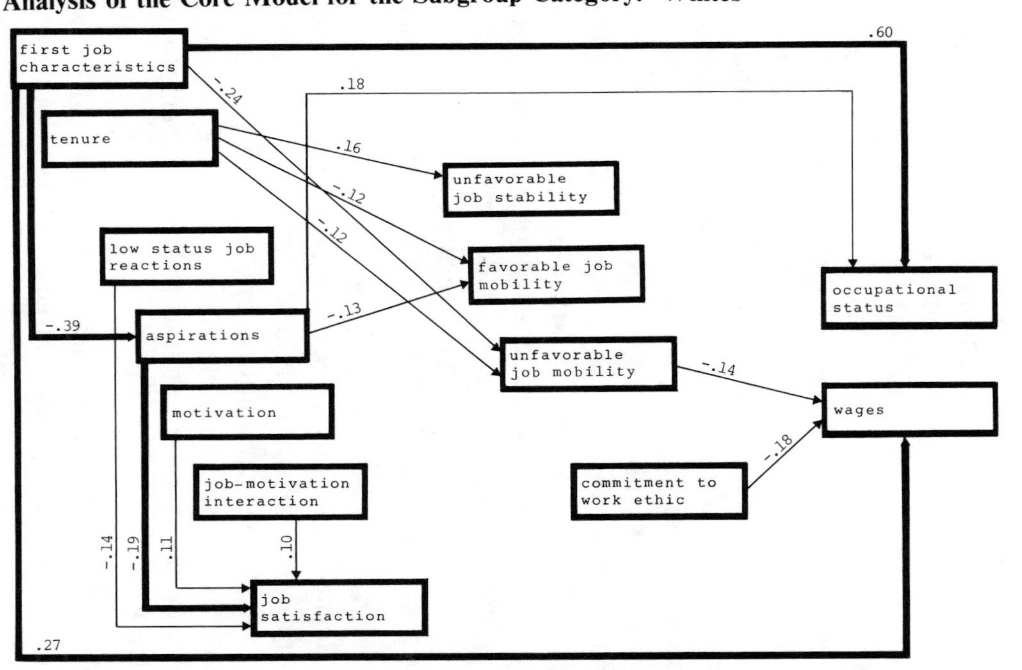

All paths indicated are significant beyond the .05 level according to the *F* ratio with N-k-1 degrees of freedom. Bold line paths are significant at .001. Path coefficients are standardized regression coefficients.

This appears to indicate that for whites, a good job and/or high aspirations in the early period can lead to positive work experiences later on in spite of possible turnover or dissatisfaction problems in the interim.

Since the prior subgroup, sex, showed such demonstrable between-category differences, it is appropriate to break down the race subgroup into sex categories in order to investigate which subgroup more persistently affects early career experiences. Breaking down the white category by sex, white males, as revealed in Appendix table A1, present a pattern much more similar to males than that of whites. In fact, only five paths are different from the general male category, four of which are simply absent. These same four in the male category, furthermore, were of a relatively low order of significance. Missing, then, in the white male analysis as compared to the male analysis are job-motivation interaction in the occupational status equation, aspirations in the wages equation, and first job characteristics and job satisfaction in the commitment equation. The new path is the negative relationship between favorable job mobility and commitment. Apparently, white males who change jobs and subsequently become satisfied with their new job do not have a great deal of respect for the work ethic and are more inclined to believe that one gets ahead through luck rather than hard work.

Compared to white youth in general, the white male results, uncontaminated by the effects of the female sample, demonstrate that job mobility and dissatisfaction can have negative effects on later employment. However, a now common theme emerges, that being that a good first job and, to a lesser extent, high aspirations lead to beneficial employment results later on.

The findings for white females, as in the case of the white males, are substantially more affected by sex than by race. Comparable to the earlier discussion with regard to the women's findings, there are a dearth of relationships in the analysis of the core model for the white women (see Appendix table A2). Again, no paths lead to later wages. First job characteristics, however, positively affect later occupational status. Unlike the general female category, aspirations do not account for any significant amount of the variance in occupational status, but they do affect job mobility-satisfaction in the middle period. The higher the aspirations of the young white female worker, the less satisfied she will be with a subsequent job, whether it be the same as her first job or a different job. On the other hand, relatively low aspirations—as most are—will result in less dissatisfaction. These findings seem to indicate that aspirations, even if formed before the first job, are certainly affected by that job. If aspirations are low, then the first and subsequent jobs will be deemed satisfactory. If, on the other hand, they are high and the first job is not of sufficient quality to match them, it can be surmised that discrimination of one kind or another will likely result in a continued state of underemployment and dissatisfaction.

Blacks

The findings for the black youth will also be viewed in terms of sexual as well as racial differences. First, general racial differences are discussed. The pattern of career development for first jobholders among blacks differs substantially from whites in both nature and magnitude (see Table 8 and Figure 6). However, the path model does not really account for the dissimilarity in labor market experience at any one point in time between these groups.

In order to examine the latter concern more closely, we can analyze the difference between whites and blacks on any of the variables used in this study. Applying an analysis of variance procedure to the principal dependent variables revealed significant differences at the .001 level. The mean

Table 8
Path Regression Results of the Analysis of the Core Model for the Subgroup Category: Blacks

Significant paths	BETA	F	DF	R	R^2
Occupational status 1975			11 99	.6850	.4693
Unfavorable job stability	-.2553	4.065			
Unfavorable job mobility	-.2608	4.257			
Aspirations	.2618	9.830			
First job characteristics	.6070	39.883			
Wages 1975			11 99	.5282	.2790
Tenure on first job	.2135	5.584			
Aspirations	.2289	5.530			
First job characteristics	.3327	8.823			
Commitment to work ethic			10 100	.4352	.1894
Unfavorable job stability	-.3285	4.659			
Aspirations	.2034	4.084			
Unfavorable job stability			7 103	.3183	.1013
Tenure on first job	.2123	4.884			
Favorable job mobility			7 103	.2104	.0442
None					
Unfavorable job mobility			7 103	.2289	.0524
None					
Job satisfaction			6 179	.4171	.1740
Aspirations	-.2280	9.507			
Low status job reactions	-.2366	11.796			
Low status job reactions			2 322	.0760	.0057
None					
Aspirations			2 183	.3430	.1176
First job characteristics	-.3054	19.265			
Tenure on first job	.1781	6.554			
Motivation			2 298	.0011	.0000
None					
Job-motivation interaction			1 325	.0146	.0002
None					

Figure 6
Analysis of the Core Model for the Subgroup Category: Blacks

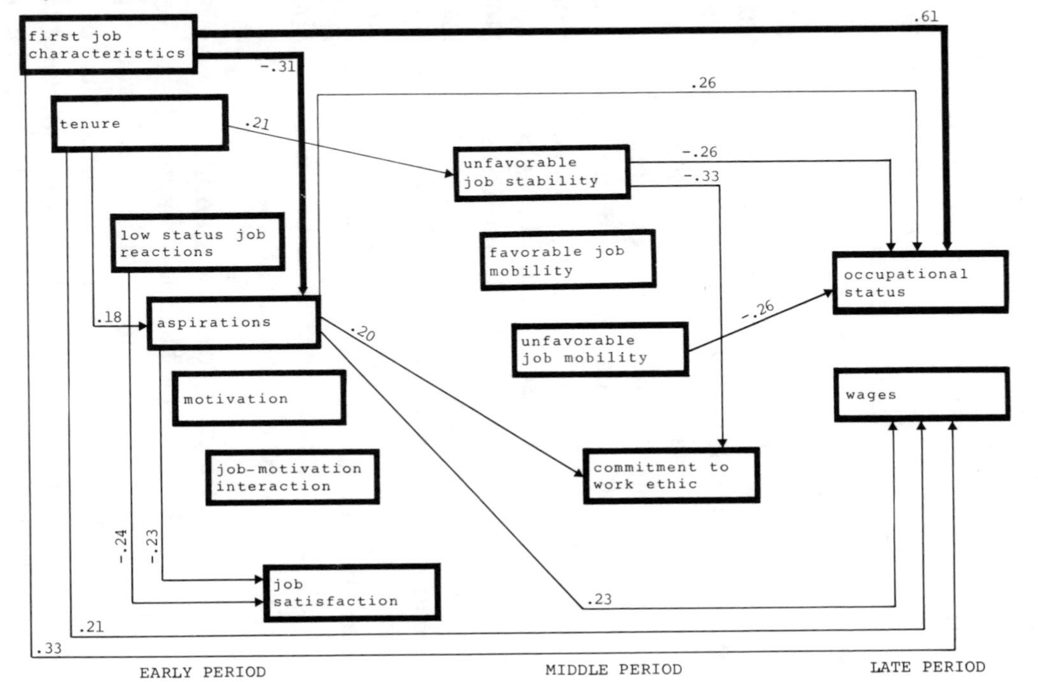

All paths indicated are significant beyond the .05 level according to the *F* ratio with N-k-1 degrees of freedom. Bold line paths are significant at .001. Path coefficients are standardized regression coefficients.

wage difference in the late period, for example, was 1,748 dollars. Further, tests for homogeneity of variances also revealed significant differences indicating that whites were less constricted in the range of occupations and salaries they could enjoy. Finally, significant mean differences between these groups were found for many of the other variables: first job characteristics, tenure, job-motivation interaction, and satisfaction, from the early period; and commitment, from the middle period. The white youth in each case obtained the higher score. However, it is important to note that no significant differences were found for *change* in either occupational status or wages between the early and late periods.

These initial findings, though not part of the core model's primary concern, as they merely demonstrate zero-order effects, do confirm well-known and well-established evidence that blacks as a racial group in our society have been relegated to the lowest positions in our economy due to any number of causes, such as education and family background, but most critically, due to outright discrimination. Further, from such authors as Hare (1965), Leiberson and Fuguitt (1967), Duncan (1968), and Ornstein (1976), we know that the racism encountered by black Americans does not descend at any one point; rather, it accumulates at each successive step of the career process. Finally, Almquist (1979) has concluded that next to American Indians, blacks are, overall, the most impoverished of the eight minority groups which she intensively studied.

Returning to the core model, the findings, as was stated earlier, are notable on the basis of magnitude as well as nature. About twice the amount of variance is accounted for by blacks as compared to whites in the equations for later wages, commitment to the work ethic, and unfavorable job stability. Although first job characteristics is the most powerful predictor, specifically in terms of later occupational status and wages, aspirations is the most pervasive. The latter appears in four of the regression equations. This means that high aspirations are very important for blacks in explaining their later occupational status and wages, their commitment, and, in a negative direction, their initial job satisfaction. Further, tenure on the first job, which is positively related to aspirations, has a high likelihood of leading to job dissatisfaction in the middle period, assuming that the first job is retained. The resultant unfavorable job stability in turn negatively affects commitment and later occupational status. These findings pull together a variety of conclusions, albeit disconnected, from other studies. From Ornstein (1976) we know that the black rate of mobility is lower than that of whites. It is reasonable to assume that this relative immobility of blacks results from a lack of opportunity in the labor market which in turn leads to insecurity. Lacking a relatively good first job, the young black's aspirations are heightened (Andrisani et al. 1977). In fact, confirming the findings of Parnes et al. (1970) and Jones (1977), blacks tend to have higher aspirations but lower immediate work expectations as compared to whites. However, as time moves on, the black worker becomes more and more dissatisfied with his/her job, and this dissatisfaction can lead to negative occupational results later on. Dissatisfaction accompanying a job resulting from a change in employers can have an equally negative consequence. In order to prosper in the work world, prosperity being relegated to only a small proportion of black workers, the young black has to secure a good stable first job and/or maintain high career aspirations without becoming overly dissatisfied.

Breaking down the young black subgroup by sex will reveal whether the effects of race are conditioned by differences attributable to sex. In the case of whites, the career patterns of youth were more affected by sex than by race.

For black males, race appears to be more significant in explaining career developments than sex, although there are some patterns peculiar to this category in its own right. Common to blacks in general, black males, in order to get ahead, need to rely on a good first job and/or high aspirations (see Appendix table A3). In fact, black male aspirations are easily the highest of all sex-race categories. However, unlike their general racial category, no particular trait can be pinpointed, such as mid-term job dissatisfaction, to account for a lack of advancement in terms of occupation or salary in the late period. Kohen et al. (1977) suggest a response for this void by showing that young male racial inequality, in terms of a number of measures of labor market success, e.g., salary, status, unemployment, or distance in occupational advancement, exceeds what can be accounted for by racial differentials in human capital. Hence, beyond such investments as schooling, young black males face unsalutary labor market effects as a result of discriminatory treatment.

Finally, unlike either males or blacks in general, black males who like their first job are more likely to sustain their satisfaction with that job if retained into the middle period but become dissatisfied if they switch jobs. This appears to signal a preference among young black males for job stability, which from what the Career Thresholds studies have been telling us, may represent a legitimate insecurity vis-a-vis the labor market.

Turning to black females, it is particularly difficult to assess whether sex or race accounts for more of their early career patterns. Contrary to Almquists's inquiry (1979), black women eventually earn slightly more than white women, even before controlling for education and occupation, but earn less than black men. However, black women, probably having completed fewer years of school, end up in lower status jobs than do white women. Finally, it has been suggested elsewhere that despite high poverty rates in addition to their low status jobs, black women have very high rates of employment. This finding contrasts with most other minority women (Almquist 1979). Cain (1966) has suggested that black women work because of financial need, or put another way, because black men have such poor success in the labor market.

In terms of later work experience, in this study the analysis of the core model for black women is hampered by the low number of cases. Nevertheless, Appendix table A4 may be consulted to indicate some likely patterns of experience in terms of work conditions and attitudes prevalent in a black woman's early career. Besides the first job, a good deal of the variance in later occupational status is accounted for by unfavorable job mobility. No predictors are found for later wages, however. Findings for commitment are perhaps most revealing. Black women, who generally have high career aspirations relative to white women, are likely to incur job transitions, presumably out of financial necessity as well as their aspirations. However, they are unlikely to be satisfied with their new job and their dissatisfaction will also affect not only their subsequent wages but their commitment to work as well. Like young white women, overall there do not appear to be a great many options available to them in mounting a successful career campaign through work-related variables, at least from what can be discerned from this small sample applied to the core model. Comparable to the previously cited findings for blacks in general, unsuccessful transitions can jeopardize their occupational advancement. The principal clues to relative success seem to be to obtain a good first job or, if lacking value, change jobs carefully while keeping one's aspirations and commitment intact, a tall task indeed.

Subgroup Analysis: Education

As the next subgroup to be examined, education is a viable candidate for separate analysis since researchers have well established its effects on work experience. Recalling chapter 2, it was mentioned that Blau and Duncan (1967) found educational attainment together with the education and occupation of the father to explain much of the variation in the quality of the first job. Ornstein (1976) found that education directly affected occupational prestige but not wages on the job held after eight years in the labor force. Kohen et al. (1977) demonstrated that schooling, formal training, and on-the-job training each had *independent* effects on later labor market success for the young male cohort of the NLS.

In this sample, breaking the education subgroup down into three categories—less than high school, high school, and college education—a range test using the Student-Neuman-Keuls procedure revealed separate significant subsets for these categories when comparing their group means on both principal dependent variables—occupational status and wages (see Table 9). It is interesting to note that means did not differ significantly when change in occupation or wages was used as the dependent variable except in the instance of college education for change in wages. In other words, education can certainly affect one's ultimate work experience, but, except where one is college-educated with respect to the wage differential, education has no significant effect in terms of the progress one makes in the labor market. This finding signifies perhaps the added importance of landing that first respectable job, which is obviously affected by education. The importance of college education, reflected in the absolute values shown in Table 9, has been sustained by Olneck (1977: chap. 6) who reported that controlling for background and test scores, returns to four years of college are likely to be somewhat higher than returns to

Table 9
Range Tests for Effect of Education on Later Work Experience Variables[a]

Education	Occupational status 1975		Wages 1975		Change in occupational status 1966-1975		Change in wages 1966-1975	
	$\bar{x}$	SNK	$\bar{x}$	SNK	$\bar{x}$	SNK	$\bar{x}$	SNK
less than high school	23.0		5558		4.3		3582	
		.05		.05		n.s.		n.s.
high school	39.9		6907		4.9		3786	
		.05		.05		n.s.		.05
college +	65.4		12037		6.8		7597	

a. Effects measured by group mean differences using the Student-Neuman-Keuls procedure.

four years of secondary school. Nevertheless, completing high school rather than elementary school is also significantly associated with subsequent economic success.

Turning to the core model of initial job experiences, the results are displayed for education in Appendix tables A5-A7 according to the three categories mentioned above. It may be of interest to point out before discussing these findings that separate regressions were run for these categories further breaking them down for the aforementioned sexual and racial categories. As might be expected, sex was a more pronounced modifier of the career patterns observed in the general education categories, although major differences were noted for women but not for men. Racial effects were not that significant. In fact, the pattern variations very much reflected the changes for the separate sex and race analyses, indicating a low likelihood of interaction effects. As a confirmatory note, Olneck's data, reported earlier, were not found to vary significantly on the basis of race. Further evidence of multiple modifier effects awaits the discussion of the full model at the end of this chapter.

Appendix table A5 displays the results of the analysis of the core model for youth with a high school education. The pattern of initial job experiences which is revealed is clearly a subset of the overall analysis of the core model, indicating that high school education represents average experience. Again first job characteristics and aspirations are important in explaining later work experience, but the mid-term mobility-satisfaction variables do not enter the occupational status or wage equations. Tenure on the first job can lead to dissatisfaction in the middle period if the first job is retained. Finally, although job satisfaction is associated with a number of career attitudes, it does not have later work attitudinal or experiential effects.

The comparison of the analysis for high school graduates to those with less than a high school education is interesting in that the latter category reveals a dearth of relationships (see Appendix table A6). Getting a good initial job seems to be the only way to break the odds against forever remaining in low level employment. This consequence can be made somewhat more palatable through increased financial remuneration, but this late period result is associated with stability on the first job. For the undereducated, it is apparent that seniority allows a modicum of subsequent extrinsic rewards from work. The quality of the undereducated youth's first job is also positively related to initial job satisfaction. However, the first job being essentially a secondary job for these youth, i.e., low level and low tenured, satisfaction is relatively low. Further, if the job has been held for only a short time and if it doesn't meet the youth's intrinsic motives, satisfaction will get no better over time. These findings, incidentally, are nearly identical for a dropout subset of the undereducated category which was formed by limiting membership to those over 18 years of age.

Interestingly enough, the theme of intrinsic motivation, alluded to above for the undereducated, appears again for the highly educated except that their intrinsic motivation is not tied to the job; rather, it is viewed as a separate concept, perhaps as an expectation. For the college educated (see Appendix table A7), the quality of the first job is positively associated with intrinsic motivation. This kind of motivation, which arises from challenge in the work being done, normally leads to tenure with the same employer and continued job satisfaction. These traits contribute to a positive commitment to the work ethic on the part of such youth. Although the work attitudes described here are interesting in their own right, perhaps shedding some new light on education as a moderator (Rabinowitz and Hall 1977), they do not participate that heavily in the later financial position of the highly educated youth, except that dissatisfaction resulting from an unsuccessful employer change can depress later earnings. However, the key factors which do lead to later financial success for these youth are also not necessarily work-related; in fact, as we shall see in the next section, they are likely to originate with family background, which does not appear in the core model. As for later occupational status, the main precursors in the educated youth analysis are first job characteristics and aspirations with the latter also operating when initial job quality is relatively low. Aspirations, however, are generally lower among the highly educated, compared to the two other education groups.

Subgroup Analysis: Socioeconomic Status

Previous investigators (e.g., Blau and Duncan 1967; Duncan, Featherman, and Duncan 1972; Sewell and Hauser 1975; and Ornstein 1976) have established the role of socioeconomic status in accounting for the subsequent quality of one's job. These researchers have also considered a greater variety of background characteristics than the one used here—father's or mother's occupation; in fact, such factors as father's and mother's education, region of birth, and family size have been included. The conclusion of this body of research seems to be that family background is important in the stratification process mostly because of its direct effect on education which, in turn, affects status and wages. Direct effects of family background on status are slight. Corcoran and Jencks (1977), incorporating an even larger number of background characteristics in their research, basically concur with these findings although they show that in addition to educational attainment, test scores and occupational aspirations also serve as intermediaries between background and later work experience.

In this sample, a oneway analysis of variance on the principal dependent variables by socioeconomic status, which was recoded into three categories, did reveal significant zero-order effects, though these were not of the magnitude of education. In fact, for both later occupational status and wages, a range test using the Student-Neuman-Keuls procedure revealed no significant differences between the middle and high socioeconomic status categories. When change in occupational status was used as a dependent variable, group mean results were reversed; in other words, the lower the socioeconomic status, the more likely one could advance in occupational status.

Analysis of the core model for socioeconomic status as a subgroup reflects the aforementioned findings in that the results are not particularly revealing except for a few points (see Appendix tables A8-A10). First job characteristics and aspirations are predominant in explaining later work experience for the low SES group. Commitment to the work ethic appears in the later wages equation for both middle and low SES categories and carries a negative sign, but it vanishes when the male subsample alone is considered. As discussed earlier, it appears to arise because women, particularly white women, having high commitment, face very high wage disparity. Although not shown in the SES tables, when the middle class category is broken down by sex, low status job reactions are found to be positively related to later occupational status for young males. This marks the first appearance of this particular attitude in any of the late period equations, indicating that middle class male youth are especially capable of overcoming the initial effects of secondary jobs.

Looking at middle period effects, the lower the initial aspirations, on the part of upper class youth, the greater the job satisfaction and the commitment to the work ethic. On the other hand, for lower class youth, the first job has more to do with one's subsequent commitment to work. Lower class youth, as a result of their relatively poor initial position, may change jobs but are likely to become dissatisfied. Hence, career aspirations play more of a role in determining mid-term attitudes for upper class youth as compared to the work itself, which is the key precursor of these attitudes for lower class youth.

Subgroup Analysis: Disadvantaged

Having explored the effects of race, education, and socioeconomic status on early career patterns of youth, it might be informative to consider the more disenfranchised categories of each of these subgroups as a proxy for disadvantagement in our society. The purpose of this examination would be to discern effects which should be understood and either reinforced or countered, whatever the case might be, by public policy.

Previous research on the disadvantaged has revealed that they possess initial work orientations similar to those of middle class Americans, but that after a period of social deprivation, they become gradually disenchanted with work (Berg 1974; Goodwin 1972). They then learn to live with reduced needs and impoverished satisfaction (Wolfbein 1967).

In this sample of youth, by categorizing according to low socioeconomic status, undereducation, or minority status, and applying the core model, an approximation can be obtained of the effects of initial job experiences and attitudes on the part of the disadvantaged. Beforehand, a comparison was made between the disadvantaged group and the rest of the sample, using oneway analysis of variance, on a number of criterion variables. The results displayed the expected differences on later and initial work experiences as well as on initial job satisfaction (see Table 10). The disadvantaged are clearly inferior on each criterion variable selected. The one exception, supporting the contention of Wolfbein (1967), is that disadvantaged youth initially have significantly higher aspirations.

In terms of the core model, the results of the analysis for the disadvantaged group are striking in that the pattern revealed by Table 11 is identical to that of the low socioeconomic status category (refer to Appendix table A8). Apparently, low SES is the dominant factor in establishing the early career patterns of disadvantaged youth. As with lower class youth, the first job is the key to the career development of the disadvantaged youngster. If it is of relatively high quality, the youth can sustain healthy attitudes and receive the benefits of favorable conditions of employment. If it is of relatively low quality, i.e., a secondary job, as most are, the youth can become disenchanted, can lose the commitment to work, and will suffer in the labor market subsequently. The latter scenario is particularly unfortunate given the prior information that disadvantaged youth generally start out with high career aspirations.

Table 10
Comparison of Disadvantaged Youth to All Others on Selected Criterion Variables

Selected criterion variables	Disadvantaged $\overline{X}$	Disadvantaged n	All others $\overline{X}$	All others n	F[a]
Occupational status 1975	34.41	565	49.33	287	91.632**
Wages 1975	6529	553	7807	276	6.551**
Commitment to work ethic	147.95	404	150.02	175	1.642
Job satisfaction	3.41	703	3.52	338	4.707*
Aspirations	14.83	392	10.51	175	5.072*

a. *F* ratio computed for oneway analysis of variance.

*Significant at <.05 level.

**Significant at < .01 level.

Table 11
Path Regression Results of the Analysis of the Core Model for the Subgroup Category: Disadvantaged

Significant paths	BETA	F	DF	R	R^2
Occupational status 1975			11 217	.6304	.3974
Aspirations	.1755	9.258			
First job characteristics	.5591	64.869			
Wages 1975			11 217	.3831	.1468
Commitment to work ethic	-.2140	10.600			
Aspirations	.1395	4.128			
First job characteristics	.3531	18.274			
Commitment to work ethic			10 218	.3004	.0903
First job characteristics	.2043	5.922			
Unfavorable job stability			7 221	.2611	.0682
Tenure on first job	.1781	7.375			
Favorable job mobility			7 221	.1503	.0226
None					
Unfavorable job mobility			7 221	.3138	.0985
First job characteristics	-.2976	13.764			
Tenure on first job	-.1643	6.487			
Job satisfaction			6 354	.3160	.0999
Aspirations	-.1903	12.733			
Low status job reactions	-.1361	7.156			
Low status job reactions			2 633	.0694	.0048
None					
Aspirations			2 371	.2925	.0856
First job characteristics	-.2914	33.898			
Motivation			2 631	.0402	.0016
None					
Job-motivation interaction			1 649	.0735	.0054
None					

Subgroup Analysis: Age

The Career Threshold studies have reviewed the effects of age on such career attributes of male youth as labor market knowledge, expectations, employment status, educational advancement, and jobs. Age has also been associated with job satisfaction (Herzberg, et al. 1957; Hulin and Smith 1965; Dubin and Porter 1974) although its range has not been restricted to youth. The satisfaction studies have been unsuccessful in isolating the direct effects of age due to the confounding effects of personality and situational variables, particularly tenure (Hunt and Saul 1975).

In this study, an *a posteriori* contrast test of means of three age categories—14-17, 18-20, 21-24—revealed significant linear relationships for later occupational status and wages, commitment, initial job satisfaction, job characteristics, and, of course, tenure. Nearly identical results were found for the education categories, previously discussed. Findings for the core model analysis by age, however, offer some additional insights (see Appendix tables A11 and A12).

The younger age category has been deleted, given the sparse number of cases which would render any interpretation suspect. Comparing the middle and older age groups, then, it is apparent that more of the variance in most of the regression equations of the core model is explained by the older group. Whereas later occupational status has the same determinants, aspirations and first job characteristics emerge as additional predictors in the older group's wage equation. Further, when only males are considered, all of the job mobility-satisfaction variables as well as initial job satisfaction enter the older group's wage equation as negative predictors. This seems to indicate that once older youth enter the labor force, their future employment is somewhat more susceptible to work related experiences than is that of their middle-age counterparts. Further, perhaps due to the fact that their first job is usually a good one, their first job is likely to lead to relative job stability. If the first job eventually becomes unsatisfactory, however, their commitment is likely to be negatively affected. The overall picture presented here is that of older youth being more sensitive to labor market experiences throughout their early career as compared to their younger counterparts. Finally, early job satisfaction of both older and middle-age youth is affected by career attitudes; however, consistent with the previous conclusion, intrinsic motivation as a precursor of satisfaction for the older youth is conditioned by the requirements of the job.

Subgroup Analysis: Urbanization

Although not as widely investigated as some of the other exogenous variables vis-a-vis worklife, urbanization could be a critical variable, particularly given the diverse migration in and out of the city that has occurred in recent years. Generally speaking, some of the available research has shown that youth in urban areas tend to be less committed to work than youth in rural areas. Kohen et al. (1977) display results indicating that urban youth are more inclined to separate without lining up another job as compared to rural youth. This might occur because urban youth obtain better-paying and more prestigious jobs (Fremon 1970; Kohen et al. 1977), or because they are less personally involved with their work (Turner and Lawrence 1965; Hulin and Blood 1968). Findings from this sample dispute the latter conclusion and support the former. Oneway analyses of variance were performed on a number of criterion variables by urbanization, which was categorized into three groups: urban, suburban, and rural (see Table 12). For the following variables, results were curvilinear with the highest value recorded for the suburban youth, followed by urban and then rural: occupational status 1975, wages 1975, commitment to the work ethic, aspirations, and first job characteristics. In the case of initial job satisfaction, urban youth were most satisfied, followed by

Table 12
Comparison Between Urban, Suburban, and Rural Youth on Selected Criterion Variables

Selected criterion variables	1. Urban $\bar{x}$	n	2. Suburban $\bar{x}$	n	3. Rural $\bar{x}$	n	Significant ranges[a]
Occupational status	40.63	346	42.97	304	33.59	448	3 ● (1,2)
Wages 1975	7434	330	7662	302	6411	432	3 ● (1,2)
Commitment to work ethic	148.70	233	149.85	193	147.70	314	none
Job satisfaction	3.45	462	3.42	382	3.93	534	none
Aspirations	13.66	251	18.67	215	12.42	319	(3,1) ● 2
First job characteristics	95.71	450	96.38	375	90.61	527	3 ● (1,2)
Tenure on first job	1.17	429	1.23	348	1.21	492	none

a. Ranges examined by *a posteriori* contrast test comparing pairs of group means. Significance established by Student-Neuman-Keuls procedure.

suburban youth; whereas for tenure, suburban youth held their jobs longest, followed by rural youth. These findings indicate that urban and suburban youth not only get better jobs but are more satisfied with their job and more committed to the work ethic. Although no firm conclusions can be drawn, it does appear that urban youth separate more readily than rural youth because they can afford to.

Analyses were performed applying the core model to categories of urbanization in order to examine whether early career patterns of youth are affected by area of residence. The results demonstrate no patterns of interest whether comparisons are made between the categories themselves or between the urbanization subgroup and the overall sample.

Subgroup Analysis: Job Level

Although participating in the core model and therefore not an exogenous variable, the volume of research on job level suggests taking a closer look at its direct effects on a youth's early career. Ornstein (1976) found the first job a youth takes after entry into the labor force to have a large effect on the job held eight years later. In particular, the wage of the first job largely determines the wage of the later job. The prestige of the first job, however, though affecting one's later job, is more closely tied to education. Kohen et al. (1977) also found work experience to have more of an independent effect on wages than prestige. With regard to effects on attitudes, research evidence now seems to suggest that any relationship to job satisfaction on the part of job level is contingent on worker aspirations, needs, and values (Kasl 1974).

In this study, an examination of the zero-order effects of job level, trichotomized from the first job characteristics variable, on each of the other variables of the core model discloses linear relationships, mostly significant, almost all of which go in the expected direction. Exceptions are for motivation and tenure wherein the middle job level takes on the lowest value in the first instance and the highest value in the second. Although not unexpected, aspirations work in reverse order; that is, the higher the job level, the lower the aspirations. The findings for job level as an independent contributor to later career development are certainly the most powerful of any single variable studied so far; nevertheless, the various subgroup analyses have demonstrated the moderating effects of other core and exogenous factors. The relative role of first job characteristics will receive additional attention in the ensuing discussion of the full model analysis.

Applying job level to the core model itself presents a few findings of note, particularly in the case of high job level (see Table 13). The data reveal the critical importance of the first job as the single significant factor positively associated with later occupational status and wages. This indicates that even

Table 13
Path Regression Results of the Analysis of the Core Model for the Subgroup Category: High Job Level

Significant paths	BETA	F	DF	R	R^2
			11		
Occupational status 1975			69	.4374	.1913
First job characteristics	.3881	9.458			
			11		
Wages 1975			69	.5279	.2786
First job characteristics	.4652	15.236			
			10		
Commitment to work ethic			70	.3175	.1008
Unfavorable job stability	-.2781	4.127			
			7		
Unfavorable job stability			73	.3182	.1012
None					
			7		
Favorable job mobility			73	.3510	.1232
First job characteristics	-.2747	5.213			
			7		
Unfavorable job mobility			73	.1528	.0233
None					
			6		
Job satisfaction			105	.3476	.1208
Job-motivation interaction	.2511	7.045			
Aspirations	-.2060	4.607			
			2		
Low status job reactions			228	.1187	.0141
None					
			2		
Aspirations			111	.2039	.0415
First job characteristics	-.2074	4.667			
			2		
Motivation			227	.1754	.0307
None					
			1		
Job-motivation interaction			230	.0492	.0024
None					

at high quality levels, distinctions can be made between just the "good" versus the "cream" jobs to the extent these distinctions lead to different results in later employment. Similarly, the "cream" jobs lead to greater stability in the middle period and, in conjunction with needs, to greater initial job satisfaction. Finally, although applying the other categories of job level to the core model analysis does not result in isolating first job characteristics as the single critical variable in explaining later work experience, it nevertheless does appear along with other factors. This appears to indicate the significance of its variability even within categories. In the case of low job level, however, it does not explain as much of the variance in later occupational status as aspirations, suggesting again how the latter in some instances can overcome initial deprived opportunity.

Subgroup Analysis: Tenure

Like job level, tenure is not an exogenous variable in the core model; rather, it is a primary descriptor of the initial job experience of youth. Nevertheless, its importance in one's early career, as established by the literature, merits its attention here as a separate subgroup. The literature has found tenure on the first job to be most significant, in terms of later work experience, for educated whites (Ornstein 1976; Kohen et al. 1977). However, Ornstein finds this effect for later wages, whereas Kohen et al. find it for later status. Further, Ornstein reports a negative relationship between tenure and wages, whereas Kohen et al. observe a positive effect on later status. A potential resolution of these conflicting findings lies in the explanation that perhaps job stable youth trade occupational status for wages.

With respect to attitudinal effects, both negative and positive relationships have been found for tenure and job satisfaction (Gibson and Klein 1970; Hunt and Saul 1975), which suggests caution in seeking a simple explanation for such effects. Similar disparities were noted earlier for age.

In order to examine the zero-order effect of tenure on the variables of the core model, oneway analyses of variance were performed based on a simple dichotomy: initial job held less than one year vs. more than one year. Contrary to Ornstein's findings, the results display positive benefits to tenure before adding any controls with one exception: job stable youth are more likely to be dissatisfied with their original job retained five years later (see Table 14). Job unstable youth are more likely to continue their job changing behavior. They will also earn less and find themselves in lower-level occupations and will not advance as much in both status and earnings as compared to job stable youth. Finally, there is virtually no difference in the initial job satisfaction enjoyed by these two groups.

The unique effects of tenure have been reviewed in the prior core model analyses and also await additional examination in the ensuing discussion of the full model. Applying tenure as a subgroup to the core model reveals one interesting set of findings. The results for those youth with under one year of tenure on their first job demonstrate the critical importance of quality of the first job (see Table 15). Other than in the instance of job satisfaction, incoming paths have first job characteristics as their sole predictor. Later occupational status and wages are very much dependent on the first job. If the job is poor, it can lead to low status job reactions or high aspirations, both of which are negatively associated with job satisfaction. A poor first job can also lead to additional job mobility which for this group will most likely lead to successive jobs which are equally unsatisfactory.

Table 14
Comparison Between Job Stable and Job Unstable Youth on Selected Criterion Variables[a]

Selected criterion variables	Job stable $\bar{x}$	Job stable n	Job unstable $\bar{x}$	Job unstable n	F[b]
Occupational status 1975	39.47	591	37.14	508	2.956*
Wages 1975	8502	565	5491	500	55.619***
Change in occupational status 1966-1975	5.49	580	4.25	506	1.073
Change in wages 1966-1975	4890	556	3240	492	19.092***
Unfavorable job stability	.34	382	.18	307	21.158***
Favorable job mobility	.21	382	.29	307	5.629**
Unfavorable job mobility	.21	382	.35	307	18.528***
Job satisfaction	3.42	752	3.43	627	.082

a. Job stability defined as greater than 1 year of tenure on first job; job instability defined as less than 1 year of tenure on first job.

b. *F* ratio computed for one-way analysis of variance.

*Significant at $< .1$ level.

**Significant at $< .05$ level.

***Significant at $< .01$ level.

Table 15
Path Regression Results of the Analysis of the Core Model for the Subgroup Category: Less than One Year of Tenure

Significant paths	BETA	F	DF	R	R^2
Occupational status 1975			10 148	.6387	.4080
First job characteristics	.5353	35.789			
Wages 1975			10 148	.2995	.0897
First job characteristics	.3191	8.269			
Commitment to work ethic			9 149	.2507	.0629
None					
Unfavorable job stability			6 152	.1397	.0195
None					
Favorable job mobility			6 152	.1510	.0228
None					
Unfavorable job mobility			6 152	.2907	.0845
First job characteristics	-.2586	6.006			
Job satisfaction			5 273	.3170	.1005
Aspirations	-.1619	6.508			
Low status job reactions	-.1676	8.327			
Low status job reactions			1 582	.0853	.0073
First job characteristics	-.0853	4.269			
Aspirations			1 290	.4083	.1667
First job characteristics	-.4083	58.031			
Motivation			1 570	.0396	.0016
None					

Full Model Analysis

Now that each of the separate subgroups have been individually examined, the full model can be revealed which entails incorporating the demographic, education, and labor market variables, described in chapter 3, into the trimmed core model. The full model will also include some exogenous variables which did not receive separate subgroup treatment. Since the full model is composed of a series of multiple regression equations, the surviving paths distinguish unique effects operating during a young person's early career.

The full model is displayed in Table 16. Discussion of the findings therein will proceed in a similar manner to that undertaken for the core model. Independent effects on the principal dependent variables will be outlined first, particularly the exogenous effects as well as changes in the core effects. This will be followed by discussion of other independent effects, of indirect effects, and of other intermediate paths.

Independent Effects

The explanation of later occupational status as revealed by the trimmed core model analysis is not greatly affected by inclusion of the exogenous variables. The only new entrant into the equation is intelligence. Further, only 3 percent more of the variance is explained in the full model for occupational status. First job characteristics continues to dominate, and middle period dissatisfaction maintains its negative association. Aspirations continues to show a strong, positive linear relationship, refuting the original hypothesis about its potential curvilinear trend. Clearly, the work experience and attitudinal factors of the core model are most significant in accounting for later status.

Table 16
Path Regression Results of the Analysis of the Full Model for the Overall Sample

Significant paths	BETA	F	DF	R	R^2
Occupational status 1975			25 398	.6840	.4679
Unfavorable job stability	-.1059	6.789			
Unfavorable job mobility	-.1211	8.724			
Aspirations	.1530	12.613			
First job characteristics	.5190	85.768			
Intelligence	.2067	20.540			
Wages 1975			25 398	.6078	.3695
Unfavorable job mobility	-.1423	10.552			
New England	-.1079	4.524			
Sex	.5682	144.612			
Age	.0977	4.549			
Schooling	.1919	17.883			
Commitment to work ethic			21 665	.4989	.2489
West South Central Region	.1012	4.404			
Sex	-.4335	145.415			
Race	.1168	7.621			
Unfavorable job stability			23 477	.2668	.0711
Tenure on first job	.1603	10.869			
Favorable job mobility			22 478	.2176	.0473
Tenure on first job	-.0999	4.129			
East North Central Region	-.1674	5.220			
Unfavorable job mobility			23 477	.2873	.0825
First job characteristics	-.1948	10.748			
Tenure on first job	-.1209	6.213			
Job satisfaction			25 494	.3883	.1508
Motivation	.1161	7.539			
Aspirations	-.1957	19.570			
Low status job reactions	-.1569	13.931			
Race	.1285	5.713			
Low status job reactions			21 721	.1229	.0151
None					

Table 16 (continued)

Significant paths	BETA	F	DF	R	R^2
Aspirations			22 497	.5243	.2748
First job characteristics	-.5790	126.014			
Community size	-.2101	10.836			
Not in central city	.1130	4.327			
Schooling	.1243	7.494			
Intelligence	.2541	30.278			
Motivation			21 721	.1716	.0294
Community size	.1453	5.710			
Sex	.1120	8.142			
Job-motivation interaction			21 721	.4998	.2498
Sex	-.1191	11.929			
Race	.2520	38.488			
Age	.1083	8.857			
Socioeconomic status	.0843	5.276			
Schooling	.1680	21.028			
Intelligence	.0880	5.326			
First job characteristics			21 721	.6720	.4515
Community size	-.1578	11.921			
East North Central Region	.1277	7.964			
South Atlantic Region	.1440	8.942			
Sex	-.0994	11.363			
Race	.1443	17.270			
Age	.2317	55.393			
Socioeconomic status	.1348	18.474			
Schooling	.2609	69.370			
Intelligence	.1847	32.031			
Tenure on first job			21 721	.4206	.1769
Sex	.2880	63.496			
Age	.3255	72.860			

The picture is altogether different for later wages. Outside of unfavorable job mobility, the other original core model factors vanish and are replaced by four exogenous factors. Three of them—sex, schooling, and age—have been shown in the subgroup analyses to significantly affect wages. The fourth, residence in the New England region, though significant at this point, will disappear under trimming. The single most important explanatory path is that of sex, which has the highest beta coefficient of all model paths. This confirms earlier reported findings of deep-seated wage discrimination at the expense of the young women population for the years studied. Particularly with the inclusion of sex in the wage equation, 37 percent of the variance is explained by the full model as compared to 13 percent by the trimmed core.

Since commitment to the work ethic has no outgoing paths, its precursors will be treated here as independent effects. Whereas in the core model, it had no significant predictors, three exogenous factors emerge in the full model analysis and explain nearly 25 percent of the variance. Of these, sex again is predominant, followed by race. These two variables, as revealed by the prior subgroup analyses, must be considered together for they support this study's finding that young women, particularly white women, are more committed to work than the other sex-race groups. Finally, it appears that young workers in the then relatively poor West South Central region of the country have higher commitment than their counterparts. The fact that commitment to the work ethic has no attitudinal precursors deters the original hypothesis that specific attitudes towards one's first job get transformed into generalized attitudes towards work, although there is some evidence for this vis-a-vis young men and the highly educated. Nevertheless, it appears that commitment derives more from sociological or economic factors than psychological dispositions.

Indirect Effects

Just as in the core model analysis, job mobility-satisfaction intervenes between tenure on the first job and later work experience. The exception is that favorable job mobility does not have an outgoing path. Nevertheless, the longer the tenure on the first job, the less likely one will enjoy a job change later on. Chances for undertaking a satisfactory job change are also lessened by residence in the East North Central region of the country. Finally, having a low quality, unstable first job will likely lead to unsatisfactory mobility which, in turn, will lead to unfavorable results in later employment.

The findings therefore sustain the subgroup analysis of tenure which disclosed positive benefits to be gained by job stability. Effects on later work experience are essentially channeled through mid-term mobility-satisfaction. Longer tenure on the first job means less instability and therefore better employment results. The one exception would be when the retained first job becomes unsatisfactory by the middle period, in which case, the otherwise favorable results could be reversed. Finally, tenure itself is principally accounted for by sex and age. Older male youth are most likely to reap the later employment rewards of first job tenure.

Not only do first job characteristics have powerful effects on later work experience, but as was mentioned, they also indirectly affect the principal dependent variables through unfavorable job mobility and aspirations. If a youth changes jobs unfavorably as a result of a bad first job, the prognosis is for an inauspicious later career. However, even with such bad initial work circumstances, the above trend can be reversed through high aspirations. Obtaining a high quality first job, then, normally is critical, but such an opportunity is not open to all youth. Clearly, older youth who have had a good deal of education and who are natively intelligent stand a better chance of landing that good first job. Next, social class is important along with race as a predictor. Further, youth who come from less populated communities are favored at job entry, particularly where residence is in the East North Central and South Atlantic regions of the U.S. Finally, female youth enjoy greater prestige in their first job as compared to men, but at no point in their career is such greater prestige converted into high wages; in fact, the reverse is true. Together, the exogenous factors cited incorporate 45 percent of the variance in first job characteristics.

The remainder of the discussion of the full model turns to the attitudes generated at the outset of a young person's career. As was indicated earlier, only aspirations, of all the early career attitudes, has any effect on later experience. Further, it is negatively associated with job satisfaction which suggests that the higher one's aspirations, the less chance he or she will like the first job. It might also indicate that the appropriate path is from job satisfaction to aspirations rather than vice versa. Besides the first job, one's aspirations are significantly affected by one's intelligence as well as formal schooling. Further, in accordance with the Hulin and Blood studies (Blood and Hulin 1967; Hulin and Blood 1968), young workers from smaller communities or from the suburbs have higher aspirations than their counterparts in the cities who are theoretically "alienated from middle class norms."

Contrary to aspirations, youth, particularly males, from larger communities are more intrinsically motivated than those from smaller communities. However, very little of the variance in motivation is explained by the model. The same is true for low status job reactions which has no one significant antecedent. Both of these career attitudes, however, along with aspirations, contribute to most of the variance explained by the model for job satisfaction. The latter is also associated with race, indicating that whites are more satisfied with their initial job than blacks. Of course, the white youth's job is likely a better job than the black's. With respect to job-motivation interaction, nearly 25 percent of the variance is explained, yet it has no subsequent effects.

Overall, early period attitudes are not much affected by work experiences; rather their antecedents are for the most part demographic. They also do not play a strong role in the full model except for aspirations. It is unfortunately conceivable that these results, or lack thereof, for the attitudinal properties occur due to lack of precision in the measurement of the respective variables.

Full Model Analysis - Trimmed

The full model was trimmed according to the same procedure as was carried out for the core model. This essentially meant resubmitting the data to regression analysis but including only significant paths from the initial full model analysis. The results are disclosed in Table 17 and Figure 7.

As was the case in the core model, trimming effects little change in the model. Only two paths are eliminated; both are region of residence dummy variables, one leading to wages 1975, the other to favorable job mobility, and are not of major importance. R-squares are not appreciably affected. A difference of slightly over 4 percent in explained wages 1975 and unfavorable job stability represents the greatest disparity in R-squares. The occupational status 1975 equation shows an R-square difference of just over 1 percent. It can be concluded, therefore, that the trimmed full model incorporates the significant relationships without further need for re-specification. It is also comforting to note, as an aside, that each of the regression equations are significant, thereby justifying the inclusion of all core model variables. The trimmed full model represents the culmination of this study's investigation of a comprehensive theory of initial job experiences and later employment, and their environmental preconditions.

Table 17
Path Regression Results of the Trimmed Analysis of the Full Model for the Overall Sample

Significant paths	BETA	F	DF	R	R^2
Occupational status 1975			5 418	.6760	.4569
Unfavorable job stability	-.1071	7.550			
Unfavorable job mobility	-.1223	9.403			
Aspirations	.1687	17.640			
First job characteristics	.5621	157.033			
Intelligence	.2039	24.998			
Wages 1975			6 609	.5732	.3285
Unfavorable job mobility	-.1341	15.987			
Sex	.5304	242.270			
Age	.1381	16.063			
Schooling	.2416	48.775			
Commitment to work ethic			3 942	.4827	.2330
West South Central Region	.0749	6.835			
Sex	-.4687	268.643			
Race	.1171	16.792			
Unfavorable job stability			1 686	.1739	.0302
Tenure on first job	.1739	21.409			
Favorable job mobility			2 685	.1243	.0154
Tenure on first job	-.1057	7.773			
Unfavorable job mobility			2 662	.2442	.0596
First job characteristics	-.1974	26.852			
Tenure on first job	-.1176	9.535			
Job satisfaction			4 730	.3458	.1195
Motivation	.1121	10.311			
Aspirations	-.2239	40.620			
Low status job reactions	-.1672	22.927			
Race	.1125	10.444			

Table 17 (continued)

Significant paths	BETA	F	DF	R	R^2
			5		
Aspirations			514	.5093	.2594
First job characteristics	-.5921	162.689			
Community size	-.1780	20.029			
Not in central city	.1317	11.581			
Schooling	.1311	9.122			
Intelligence	.2338	30.943			
			2		
Motivation			1298	.1179	.0139
Community size	.0688	6.225			
Sex	.0918	11.061			
			6		
Job-motivation interaction			736	.4890	.2391
Sex	-.1190	12.970			
Race	.2347	40.318			
Age	.1064	9.920			
Socioeconomic status	.0910	6.520			
Schooling	.1753	24.320			
Intelligence	.0922	6.048			
			9		
First job characteristics			733	.6640	.4409
Community size	-.1740	34.435			
East North Central Region	.0784	7.453			
South Atlantic Region	.0919	9.305			
Sex	-.0951	11.213			
Race	.1280	15.275			
Socioeconomic status	.1319	18.007			
Age	.2245	59.649			
Schooling	.2564	69.282			
Intelligence	.1864	33.044			
			2		
Tenure on first job			1266	.4012	.1610
Sex	.2789	114.558			
Age	.3351	163.357			

Figure 7
Trimmed Analysis of the Full Model for the Overall Sample

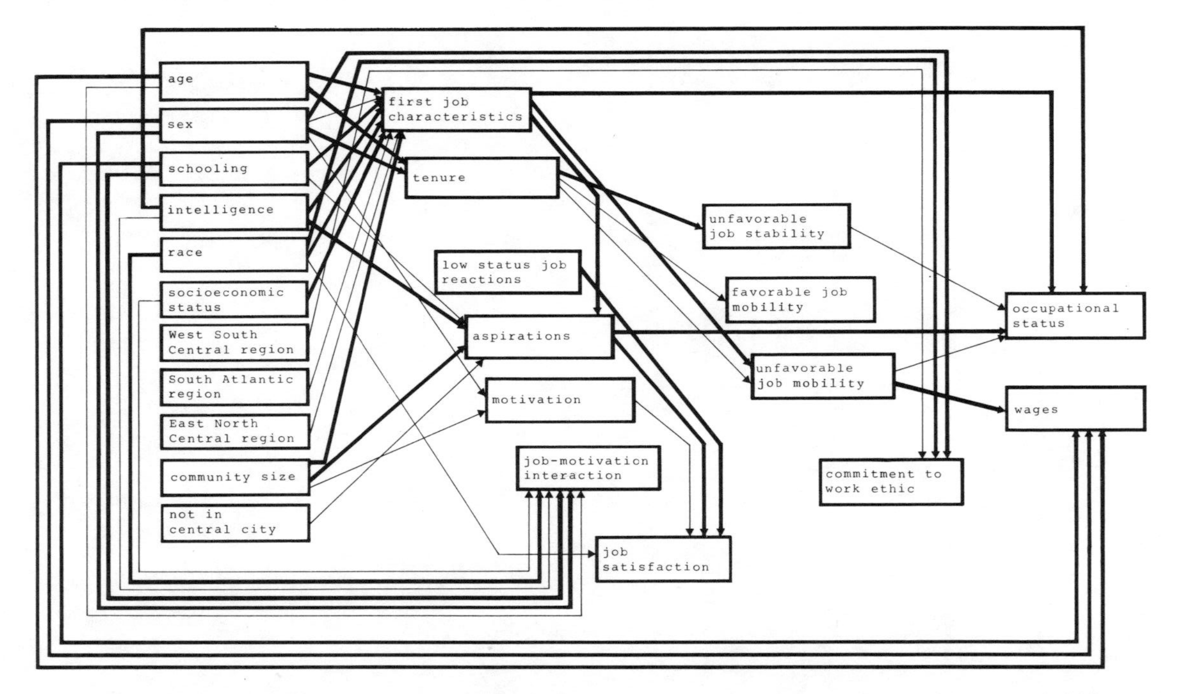

All paths indicated are significant beyond the .05 level according to the *F* ratio with N-k-1 degrees of freedom. Bold line paths are significant at .001. Path coefficients are standardized regression coefficients.

Chapter 5
Summary and Recommendations

In this chapter the findings from both the analyses of the core and full model are summarized and then outlined in capsular form. Implications are thereupon drawn for public policy on youth employment.

The premise of the study was that initial job experiences and attitudes of young people are critical in shaping their ultimate employment experience. The data base was the youth cohorts of the National Longitudinal Surveys which was refined to include only employed, out-of-school first job holders of both men and women who had been on the job for no more than seven years. The study was longitudinal in character such that the sample data were examined at three different times, approximately in 1966, 1971, and 1975. The research design centered around a path model, referred to as the "core model," which hypothesized a set of multiple, recursive relationships among a set of time-specific, work-related variables which were expressly selected because of their expected contribution to a theory of initial job experiences and later employment. The core model called for examination of early job characteristics, attitudes, and their interrelationship, intermediate work experience and attitudes, and finally later job characteristics.

The core model was not expected in and of itself to explain most of the variance in later job characteristics since there are a variety of demographic, educational, and labor market factors which affect career development apart from work experience. These so-called exogenous factors were examined in separate subgroup analyses of the core model. They were then incorporated into a full model which was constructed to explain the relative role of initial job experiences in conjunction with environmental preconditions in accounting for later employment.

Summary of Findings

The summary of findings will proceed by reviewing the results of the core model and full model analyses according to the pattern laid out in the Introduction. Early period interrelationships among experiential and attitudinal properties are considered first, followed by effects on middle period variables, finally building to direct and indirect effects on the work experience indicators of the late period.

Early Period

The first job obtained by a youngster is largely determined by his/her background, including such aspects as schooling, followed by age, intelligence, social class, and race. Youth in smaller size communities, particularly in the suburbs, and in the East generally, have the best chances of obtaining good jobs. Women initially get higher prestige jobs than men but earn lower wages. With regard to tenure on the first job, older male youth have the highest likelihood of gaining stability.

Early attitudinal reactions to employment are surprisingly, with the exception of aspirations, not greatly affected by the quality of the first job; rather their antecedents are also better explained by background factors and other career attitudes. Therefore, it can be concluded that career attitudes are substantially formed prior to the first job itself.

Aspirations constitute a different case entirely. They are significantly and negatively associated with job level. Nevertheless, they also have demographic antecedents; they tend to be higher among men, among the more intelligent and educated, among those outside of our urban areas, and finally among the disadvantaged, particularly blacks.

Initial job satisfaction is very much a product of career attitudes. Low status, secondary jobs will produce reactions strongly associated with job dissatisfaction. The higher one's aspirations, the greater the job dissatisfaction as well. In fact, a bad job with its accompanying dissatisfaction may incite higher aspirations. Finally, obtaining a match between the job and one's needs affects satisfaction slightly more than the job does by itself. Besides these attitudinal precursors, whites and women tend to be more satisfied than their counterparts.

Middle Period

An important concern in the middle period of a youth's early career is whether he or she has stayed with the initial job or changed jobs. Overall, it pays to stay with the first job unless it becomes unsatisfying. Unfortunately, if the initial job held for a relatively short time has also been a bad job, the more chances there are that the youngster will also be dissatisfied with a job change.

A scenario developed from the subgroup analyses serves to elaborate on these general findings. Basically, the disadvantaged of the youth population, including those in the lower socioeconomic class, blacks, the undereducated, or dropouts, start off as we have seen with poorer jobs. However, their options are no better if they make a job change which will likely turn out unfavorably, presumably due to poor job search skills or simply limited opportunities. Either way, their prospects for later employment success are bleak unless they can somehow build up their aspirations. There is evidence, further, that if the disadvantagement comes from undereducation, the youth may be better advised to hold onto the first job as his or her best alternative, at least to build up equity, thereby increasing the odds for earning a decent living later on.

While initial job characteristics affect mid-term mobility-satisfaction more than attitudes do, there are instances of the latter effect. For example, young white women are likely to be more favorably disposed to a mid-term job change if their aspirations are low. This is likely to be the case given that young women tend to adjust faster than men to their work due to lower expectations. On the other hand, having high aspirations will likely produce mid-term job dissatisfaction on the part of white women since the opportunities for productive work are so narrow. Contrary to the original hypothesis about aspirations, however, these high aspirations are seen as being ultimately positive. Black women essentially confront the same situation except their aspirations are higher than the white woman's (perhaps due to economic necessity), which induces them all the more to make job changes. However, these work transitions are unlikely to pay off and also negatively affect their commitment to work in general. Finally, educated youth, being very much intrinsically motivated, tend to face challenge and responsibility in their first job as a result of which they continue to stay with their first employer, sustaining a relatively high degree of satisfaction and commitment. As long as they don't make an unfavorable job change, their prospects for financial success in work remain bright.

The core model originally proposed that commitment, as a generalized work attitude, could be derived from specific job attitudes emanating from an initial job experience. Only slight evidence is found for this set of relationships—among the male and highly educated youth. Commitment is more strongly explained by sex, women being the most committed to the work ethic. In addition, along with having greater aspirations, youth from outside the urban area tend to be more committed than urban youth.

Late Period

Overall, in the late period of one's early career, occupational status seems to be more affected by prior work experience, whereas wages are mostly demographically determined. Attitudes, with the exception of initial aspirations and mid-term job dissatisfaction, do not significantly affect later employment.

There is no substitute for obtaining a good first job as the one way to insure success in employment in later years. This is particularly the case for later occupational status. Slight variations in the quality of the first job are even important since among high-level jobs, there are distinctive "cream" jobs which will lead to better results than simply "good" jobs. Obtaining a low-level first job is inauspicious in terms of later employment except that one can usually count on gaining some ground in terms of occupational status.

As indicated in the early period, there are a multitude of background factors which condition the opportunity to obtain a good job at entry. Similar factors operate to enhance the probability of being at a good job later on. Intelligence, including world of work knowledge, has a measurable effect on later occupational status, whereas age and schooling influence one's later wages. However, the one way to get an immediate advantage in terms of later wages is to not be born female. Not only are the young woman's chances of earning a subsequent salary comparable to the young man's almost nil, but she also has little chance of improving her salary position over the years relative to the man. However, she does not face this blatant discrimination vis-a-vis occupational status. This latter finding, assuming accuracy of the Duncan Index to pick up fine prestige differences between the sexes, emphasizes all the more the inequity faced by young women in the work world. In fact, women basically follow an alternate career track which, compared to men, is noteworthy in the lack of options which are available to them throughout their career and regardless of their attitudes.

Blacks and lower class youth are also at a considerable disadvantage in terms of later employment. However, the differential between them and their more privileged counterparts at least does not increase over time. In fact, lower class youth can make up some of the initial differences in occupational status.

Returning to attitudes, initial career aspirations can be critical in accounting for later employment success. Unlike what was suggested in the initial hypothesis, they have no threshold above which their utility declines. The higher the aspirations the greater the chance for obtaining a high-level job later on. Finally, aspirations are so important that they constitute one definite way to overcome a low-level first job with respect to later employment. The process is not automatic, however. Young women or undereducated youth, whose career opportunities are limited, do not tend to have high aspirations.

No other initial attitudes, including job satisfaction, account for later employment. The one exception found is for middle class male youth who are found to be able to overcome low status job reactions in order to locate more productive work later on. Otherwise, the role of initial attitudes is minimal. One explanation for this beyond a theoretical interpretation is that the measurement of attitudes, job satisfaction for example, was imprecise. Not only was it measured by a single indicator, but its distribution was highly skewed to the positive end, supporting a hypothesis of Kahn (1972) that the job satisfaction question potentially strikes too closely to one's self-esteem to be answered in an interpretable way.

With respect to the question of mobility, the overall message from the findings is that if you have a good first job, keep it. This is particularly the case for older youth who are acutely sensitive to job experiences. Unlike their younger counterparts, their initial satisfaction is dependent on motivation only to the extent that their needs are in tune with the requirements of the job. As long as the first job is satisfactory, they seem to enjoy relative job stability. However, they are very capable of becoming dissatisfied and losing their otherwise strong commitment to work if things don't go smoothly.

Overall, it appears that job dissatisfaction in the middle period, regardless of mobility, can detrimentally affect later occupational status. Therefore, job changes appear to pay off in terms of status only when they are accompanied by job satisfaction. If a youth changes jobs and becomes dissatisfied, however, an occurrence which might be precipitated by a low-level, low-tenured first job, then he or she will likely face negative consequences in wages as well as in status.

The hypothesis introduced in chapter 1 that commitment is intervening between initial job experiences and attitudes and later work experience cannot be altogether rejected for either male or college-educated youth. There is some evidence that initial job satisfaction leads to commitment which leads to wages, although the latter relationship in the sequence is not significant. However, when viewing the youth population as a whole, the intervening concept does not hold and is clearly due to the contaminating effect of the young women. They have relatively high commitment, but since their ultimate wages are so low, when combined into the total population, the effect appears to be that high commitment is negatively associated with wages.

Summary Capsule

The above summary of findings is sufficiently rich in demographic detail to perhaps blur an overview of the central findings. These are listed below.

1. The quality of a youth's first job at entry to the labor force is largely determined by background factors, particularly education.

2. Likewise, initial career attitudes are also dependent on background factors except aspirations, which run in reverse to job level.

3. Initial job satisfaction is very much a product of such career attitudes as low status job reactions, motivation, or need satisfaction. Further, job satisfaction also runs counter to aspirations.

4. A high quality first job should be held by a youth unless it become unsatisfactory or unless he or she can find a better job, in which case a change should be made. A low quality first job which has been held for only a short time, a condition typical of disadvantaged youth in the secondary labor market, will likely lead to an unfavorable job change which in turn will negatively affect later employment.

5. In the late period of one's early career, a youth's occupational status will be mostly affected by prior work experience, particularly the level of one's first job. The only way to overcome the negative effects of a low-level first job is to have high career aspirations.

6. Wages in the later period of one's career are primarily demographically determined. Young women face incredible barriers in terms of obtaining wage parity with young men. Blacks are also at a distinct disadvantage. A good education is a sure way of improving one's chances for higher earnings later on.

7. Young women, whether black or white, face an alternate career track from men which is unfortunately characterized by a dearth of opportunity to advance career-wise through work-related options. There is evidence, therefore, that sex discrimination occurs as a process throughout a career.

8. For male and college-educated youth, commitment is somewhat intervening between initial job attitudes and later employment, indicating that specific positive satisfaction from a job can become generalized into a commitment to work, which can be important in terms of later productive work experience. However, since young women are highly committed to work but underprivileged in terms of later wages, the intervening effect is lost when considering the entire youth population.

9. Psychological properties, particularly initial attitudes, do not impact on later work experience as much as economic and sociological factors. However, this may result from a lack of precision in measuring the psychological dispositions.

Recommendations

The findings are interpreted below in terms of implications for public policy on youth employment. The recommendations refer to youth employment as opposed to unemployment. Since the sample was composed of working youth out-of-school, the study bears little consequence in terms of such questions as how to narrow the unemployment rate of the youth population or its subpopulations, how to improve the transition from school to work, or how to improve initial job search activities. Rather the focus of this set of recommendations is on how to improve employment, more specifically, how to ensure that a young person gets the most out of his or her early career.

1. Once a youth finishes school, all institutions of our society that have anything to do with youth should be aligned to insure that the youth obtains the best possible job at entry. We can begin this task by starting to collect information on new youth entrants to employment. Right now, we don't even know how many youth start work at any one point in time, where they locate their first job, or what work they're doing. This data could be critical, however, particularly if organized longitudinally. For example, macro human resource planners would benefit greatly from knowing which jobs typically are taken as first jobs and among these, which ones have high or low turnover rates. Jobs with high turnover would then be examined to determine if they served a useful transition purpose or not. Identified secondary jobs should be isolated for redesign.

At the micro level, human resource managers should be held responsible for insuring that each job under their purview is useful and productive. Where subsidized jobs are created, as in public service employment programs provided under the Comprehensive Employment and Training Act (CETA), or in shorter term work experience opportunities afforded, for example, through the Summer Youth Employment Program, criteria for productiveness in work should be no less severe. It has long been speculated that such criteria are met more adequately in the private sector due to the profit motive. Whether or not this be the case, private employers and unions should be considered partners with government in the provision of adequate entry-level employment for youth. Such programs as the Private Sector Initiative Program using private industry councils or the Targeted Tax Credit are encouraged in this regard, for they encourage private sector parties to become active participants rather than just advisors to public policy.

2. Employers tend to use schooling as a screening device, therefore youth should be widely encouraged to finish school, not only as a way to get a good job, but as a way to ensure later employment success. It is certainly practical to provide work experience and training to some youth who are not academically inclined, but to the extent possible, such programs should not take the place of formal education. The latter is sufficiently important that it may pay in the long run to subsidize or provide some kind of incentive to youth to finish school while participating in work experience programs. A recent demonstration, the Youth Incentive Entitlement Pilot Projects (YIEPP), begun in 1977 by the Labor Department under the Youth Employment and Demonstration Projects Act, attempted to accomplish the foregoing objective. The YIEPP guaranteed a critically disadvantaged youth a job, part time during the school year and full time in the summer, provided he or she returned to or enrolled in school or a GED program. The implementation of the YIEPP and other such programs should be carefully evaluated to determine whether a guaranteed job or some other type of experience is the appropriate incentive to induce dropouts to return to school.

Finally, it appears that the more schooling a youth gets after high school, the more intrinsically motivated and committed he or she will be. Therefore, beyond basic and high school education, postgraduate programs should be viewed by counselors as viable alternatives to immediate job entry.

3. Beyond formal education, world of work knowledge can be instrumental in helping a youth find a productive first job and/or gainful later employment. Career exploration programs, where they haven't already, should become a part of the traditional curriculum in schools and should be incorporated into subsidized work experience or training programs. The VEPS Program—Vocational Exploration in the Private Sector—a component of the Summer Youth Employment Program co-sponsored by business and labor groups, has had success along these lines. VEPS acquaints young people with opportunities existing in the private sector. Preliminary reports are that VEPS participants undergo positive attitudinal changes, indicating initial support for this kind of programming.

4. Due to any number of background factors, youth come to work with certain expectations and motives. These motives are particularly important to educated older youth. Human resource managers, particularly recruiters, should be encouraged to talk to youth about their expectations. Jobs should be suggested which conform as much as possible to the youth's needs, within limits, acknowledging that the job finding process is a two-way street. In the manpower delivery system in CETA programs, this type of activity, oftentimes referred to as Assessment, should receive increased attention. Supervisors, if unaware of this psychological approach to work, should be oriented to it so as to provide their young subordinates with the most challenging work experiences available.

5. Since by far the most important attitude uncovered by this study in terms of its contribution to later work experience is career aspirations, every effort should be made to have the young person develop and sustain such aspirations throughout his/her early career. Having relatively poor jobs

initially, disadvantaged youth may find aspirations to be the one way to turn things around. Black youth fortunately start out with relatively high aspirations. Besides career education and counseling, big brother/big sister and other such volunteer programs demonstrating strong role models to disadvantaged youth are helpful in developing positive career aspirations. The television medium can also be helpful, as it has begun to be, in role modeling. Finally, it appears that there is no disutility to exaggerated aspirations—the higher the better. Therefore, parents and teachers, employers and friends should avoid the practice of totally discouraging so-called "impractical" aspirations.

6. There are unfortunately certain subgroups of the youth population who despite any kind of positive work disposition or experience nevertheless face severe inequity in the labor market. The most deprived group of all in terms of ultimate wage discrimination is women. They not only suffer wage disparity at the outset of their career, but unlike any other group, the wage differential as compared to their categorical counterpart, young men, widens with time. Further, their career path is noteworthy for the lack of options available to them as they pursue their ambitions, which are expected to grow over the years. Black youth, particularly men, face substantial employment discrimination relative to whites, and this finding is especially tragic given their relatively high aspirations. For these subgroups, there can be no substitute but to vigorously pursue and enforce equal employment opportunity guidelines and regulations. EEO policies are particularly indicated given that employment differentials occur throughout the career process even when background factors are controlled.

The fact that labor market opportunities may have expanded for these disadvantaged subgroups in recent years, as compared to the time period of the study, does not lessen the need for our youth employment policy to provide decent work experiences for those who are so inclined. Further, a number of obstacles still, by all accounts, have to be overcome before discrimination is eradicated in the labor market. Therefore, besides EEO policies, targeting should continue to be used in government employment and training programs; that is, certain disadvantaged subgroups should be singled out for aid. Targeting criteria should obviously include the traditional economic indicators, but racial disadvantagement should be equally considered.

7. There appears to be inefficiency in the mobility process, particularly among those who make a change from a low-level first job. This appears to be the case for disadvantaged youth, including those in the lower socioeconomic class, blacks, the undereducated, or dropouts. However, college trained, highly motivated older youth can also suffer from unsatisfactory job transitions. Career education components in school, in training programs, or even in subsidized employment should equip youngsters with job mobility skills so that they can learn to make successful transitions. Youth should receive instruction, for example, in applying job search skills to explore new situations. They should learn how to methodically evaluate a variety of career options. Employers should be encouraged to support career growth through internal advancement programs, posting, and the like, as well as through careful assessment and recruitment at the front end. Finally, since the evidence from this study backs up the secondary labor market hypothesis, a principal concern of youth employment policy should be to continue to eradicate or redesign dead-end jobs, i.e., jobs with no built-in career ladders.

8. It does not appear that resources would be well allocated if directed towards attitude change programs in place of

career enrichment, for example. In fact, before initiating more attitude programs, it would now seem necessary to concentrate more on basic and applied research with respect to the effects of attitude change on ultimate employment behavior. We have a good appreciation for what causes attitudes, but the next path, from attitudes to behavior, is tenuous in the employment sector. Basic research would refine our measurement of such constructs as job satisfaction and commitment or utilize the more advanced indicators which have been developed but with the purpose of establishing the conditions wherein early work attitudes affect long term employment. Given the present research, the only attitude worth devoting considerable practical attention to is aspirations, as was indicated earlier.

9. Youth employment research which utilizes a general sample should absolutely control for sex, followed by race and education. There are also interesting distinctions among age categories of youth. Sex is sufficiently critical, however, that research on young women should parallel any major study organized initially just for young men. There should also be an attempt to develop like measures between men and women, particularly with respect to occupational status and responsibility.

APPENDIX

APPENDIX A

Table A1
Path Regression Results of the Analysis of the Core Model for the Subgroup Category: White Males

Significant paths	BETA	F	DF	R	R^2
			11		
Occupational status 1975			251	.5880	.3458
Unfavorable job mobility	-.1511	4.873			
Aspirations	.1460	6.411			
First job characteristics	.5400	68.297			
			11		
Wages 1975			251	.5356	.2869
Unfavorable job stability	-.1834	6.805			
Favorable job mobility	-.2254	11.190			
Unfavorable job mobility	-.2169	9.206			
Job satisfaction	-.1291	4.990			
First job characteristics	.5280	59.899			
Commitment to			10		
work ethic			252	.2621	.0687
Favorable job mobility	-.1620	4.520			
Tenure on first job	.1279	4.062			
			7		
Unfavorable job stability			270	.2509	.0629
Job-motivation interaction	-.1400	4.141			
First job characteristics	.1651	5.129			
Tenure on first job	.1451	5.761			
			7		
Favorable job mobility			270	.1589	.0252
None					
			7		
Unfavorable job mobility			270	.3108	.0966
First job characteristics	-.2946	16.946			
Tenure on first job	-.1189	4.019			
			6		
Job satisfaction			390	.3653	.1334
Motivation	.1640	11.790			
Aspirations	-.2040	15.575			
Low status job reactions	-.1788	14.057			
			2		
Low status job reactions			414	.0601	.0036
None					

Table A1 (continued)

Significant paths	BETA	F	DF	R	R^2
Aspirations			2 394	.3630	.1317
First job characteristics	-.3451	52.31			
Motivation			2 424	.0488	.0023
None					
Job-motivation interaction			1 416	.0413	.0017
None					

Key to path regression tables

Only paths significant at the .05 level according to the *F* ratio with N-k-1 degrees of freedom are reported.

BETA column lists the standardized partial-regression coefficients.

F column represents the *F* ratio for each individual independent variable with 1 and N-k-1 degrees of freedom.

DF are the degrees of freedom for the entire regression run including all paths. Therefore, they contain k independent variables in the equation with degrees of freedom N-k-1.

R is the multiple correlation coefficient for the entire equation.

R^2 is the coefficient of determination or the ratio of the amount of variance in the dependent variable explained by the independent variables in the equation.

Table A2
Path Regression Results of the Analysis of the Core Model for the Subgroup Category: White Females

Significant paths	BETA	F	DF	R	R^2
			11		
Occupational status 1975			21	.7031	.4944
First job characteristics	.8074	11.678			
			11		
Wages 1975			21	.3761	.1414
None					
			10		
Commitment to work ethic			22	.3528	.1245
None					
			7		
Unfavorable job stability			25	.1988	.0395
None					
			7		
Favorable job mobility			25	.5495	.3019
Aspirations	-.6656	10.085			
			7		
Unfavorable job mobility			25	.4837	.2339
Aspirations	.5080	5.353			
			6		
Job satisfaction			87	.3069	.0942
None					
			2		
Low status job reactions			430	.0473	.0022
None					
			2		
Aspirations			92	.5847	.3418
First job characteristics	-.5921	47.690			
			2		
Motivation			432	.0684	.0046
None					
			1		
Job-motivation interaction			447	.0410	.0016
None					

Table A3
Path Regression Results of the Analysis of the Core Model for the Subgroup Category: Black Males

Significant paths	BETA	F	DF	R	R^2
Occupational status 1975			11 63	.6887	.4744
Aspirations	.2832	7.840			
First job characteristics	.6320	37.179			
Wages 1975			11 63	.5919	.3504
Aspirations	.2316	4.243			
First job characteristics	.3611	9.818			
Commitment to work ethic			10 64	.4559	.2078
None					
Unfavorable job stability			7 67	.4037	.1630
Job satisfaction	-.2728	4.778			
Favorable job mobility			7 67	.2540	.0645
None					
Unfavorable job mobility			7 67	.3090	.0955
Job satisfaction	.2508	3.739			
Job satisfaction			6 106	.4449	.1980
Motivation	.2259	6.391			
Aspirations	-.2847	9.851			
Low status job reactions			2 148	.1478	.0218
None					
Aspirations			2 110	.2531	.0640
First job characteristics	-.1971	4.521			
Motivation			2 136	.0616	.0038
None					
Job-motivation interaction			1 147	.0210	.0004
None					

Table A4
Path Regression Results of the Analysis of the Core Model for the Subgroup Category: Black Females

Significant paths	BETA	F	DF	R	R^2
			11		
Occupational status 1975			24	.7153	.5116
Unfavorable job mobility	-.6069	6.682			
First job characteristics	.7330	8.210			
			11		
Wages 1975			24	.6227	.3878
None					
			10		
Commitment to work ethic			25	.5235	.2740
Favorable job mobility	-.5677	4.309			
Aspirations	.6106	5.489			
			7		
Unfavorable job stability			28	.3877	.1503
None					
			7		
Favorable job mobility			28	.3071	.0943
None					
			7		
Unfavorable job mobility			28	.3049	.0929
None					
			6		
Job satisfaction			58	.4102	.1682
Low status job reactions	-.3205	7.063			
			2		
Low status job reactions			167	.0392	.0015
None					
			2		
Aspirations			70	.5284	.2792
First job characteristics	-.5262	25.748			
Tenure on first job	.2272	4.803			
			2		
Motivation			154	.0555	.0030
None					
			1		
Job-motivation interaction			176	.1153	.0132
None					

Table A5
Path Regression Results of the Analysis of the Core Model for the Subgroup Category: High School Education

Significant paths	BETA	F	DF	R	R^2
Occupational status 1975			11 235	.5616	.3154
Aspirations	.2038	11.027			
First job characteristics	.5371	63.338			
Wages 1975			11 235	.3306	.1093
Commitment to work ethic	-.1894	9.251			
First job characteristics	.2416	9.849			
Commitment to work ethic			10 236	.1488	.0221
None					
Unfavorable job stability			7 239	.2181	.0476
Tenure on first job	.1774	7.656			
Favorable job mobility			7 239	.1184	.0140
None					
Unfavorable job mobility			7 239	.2611	.0682
First job characteristics	-.1984	6.703			
Tenure on first job	-.1573	6.150			
Job satisfaction			6 392	.3940	.1552
Job-motivation interaction	.1225	5.448			
Motivation	.1535	10.797			
Aspirations	-.2441	22.914			
Low status job reactions	-.1785	14.641			
Low status job reactions			2 765	.0445	.0020
None					
Aspirations			2 396	.3970	.1576
First job characteristics	-.3913	70.297			
Motivation			2 759	.0516	.0027
None					
Job-motivation interaction			1 774	.0273	.0008
None					

Table A6
Path Regression Results of the Analysis of the Core Model for the Subgroup Category: Less Than High School Education

Significant paths	BETA	F	DF	R	R^2
			11		
Occupational status 1975			108	.4568	.2087
First job characteristics	.4095	15.322			
			11		
Wages 1975			108	.4401	.1937
Tenure on first job	.2129	5.613			
			10		
Commitment to work ethic			109	.3591	.1289
None					
			7		
Unfavorable job stability			112	.3589	.1288
Job-motivation interaction	-.1950	4.101			
First job characteristics	.2831	7.785			
Tenure on first job	.2012	5.115			
			7		
Favorable job mobility			112	.2731	.0745
None					
			7		
Unfavorable job mobility			112	.2445	.0598
None					
			6		
Job satisfaction			203	.3092	.0956
First job characteristics	.2259	9.041			
			2		
Low status job reaction			304	.0857	.0073
None					
			2		
Aspirations			207	.2175	.0473
First job characteristics	-.2190	10.264			
			2		
Motivation			296	.0706	.0049
None					
			1		
Job-motivation interaction			309	.0161	.0002
None					

Table A7
Path Regression Results of the Analysis of the Core Model for the Subgroup Category: College Education +

Significant paths	BETA	F	DF	R	R^2
			11		
Occupational status 1975			45	.5352	.2864
Aspirations	.6433	9.580			
First job characteristics	.8106	11.439			
			11		
Wages 1975			45	.4337	.1881
Unfavorable job mobility	-.3235	4.218			
			10		
Commitment to work ethic			46	.4106	.1686
Unfavorable job stability	-.4118	5.657			
			7		
Unfavorable job stability			49	.5209	.2713
Motivation	-.2920	5.228			
First job characteristics	.6798	10.910			
			7		
Favorable job mobility			49	.3650	.1332
None					
			7		
Unfavorable job mobility			49	.1873	.0351
None					
			6		
Job satisfaction			69	.4722	.2229
Aspirations	-.4714	8.440			
			2		
Low status job reactions			110	.0877	.0077
None					
			2		
Aspirations			73	.7338	.5385
First job characteristics	-.7382	85.148			
			2		
Motivation			110	.2277	.0519
First job characteristics	.2213	5.614			
			1		
Job-motivation interaction			111	.0835	.0070
None					

Table A8
Path Regression Results of the Analysis of the Core Model for the Subgroup Category: Low Socioeconomic Status

Significant paths	BETA	F	DF	R	R^2
Occupational status 1975			11 181	.6481	.4200
Aspirations	.1888	9.251			
First job characteristics	.5674	56.319			
Wages 1975			11 181	.3939	.1551
Commitment to work ethic	-.2180	9.191			
Aspirations	.1583	4.466			
First job characteristics	.3753	16.918			
Commitment to work ethic			10 182	.3124	.0976
First job characteristics	.2242	5.865			
Unfavorable job stability			7 185	.2797	.0782
Tenure on first job	.1890	7.051			
Favorable job mobility			7 185	.1679	.0282
None					
Unfavorable job mobility			7 185	.3304	.1092
First job characteristics	-.3216	13.452			
Tenure on first job	-.1520	4.718			
Job satisfaction			6 305	.3047	.0928
Aspirations	-.1733	8.996			
Low status job reactions	-.1374	6.230			
Low status job reactions			2 561	.0532	.0028
None					
Aspirations			2 317	.2968	.0880
First job characteristics	-.2985	30.564			
Motivation			2 558	.0441	.0019
None					
Job-motivation interaction			1 575	.0741	.0054
None					

Table A9
Path Regression Results of the Analysis of the Core Model for the Subgroup Category: Middle Socioeconomic Status

Significant paths	BETA	F	DF	R	R^2
Occupational status 1975			11 75	.6325	.4001
First job characteristics	.5388	16.235			
Wages 1975			11 75	.4780	.2285
Commitment to work ethic	-.2306	4.913			
Commitment to work ethic			10 76	.2240	.0502
None					
Unfavorable job stability			7 79	.2966	.0879
None					
Favorable job mobility			7 79	.2145	.0460
None					
Unfavorable job mobility			7 79	.2617	.0685
None					
Job satisfaction			6 115	.3787	.1434
Aspirations	-.2267	4.626			
Low status job reactions	-.1755	4.119			
Low status job reactions			2 208	.0371	.0013
None					
Aspirations			2 122	.5651	.3193
First job characteristics	-.5735	55.341			
Motivation			2 211	.0547	.0030
None					
Job-motivation interaction			1 216	.0555	.0030
None					

Table A10
Path Regression Results of the Analysis of the Core Model for the Subgroup Category: High Socioeconomic Status

Significant paths	BETA	F	DF	R	R^2
Occupational status 1975			11 49	.6640	.4409
Aspirations	.3233	4.626			
First job characteristics	.6445	21.650			
Wages 1975			11 49	.4385	.1923
First job characteristics	.3823	5.273			
Commitment to work ethic			10 50	.4038	.1630
Aspirations	-.3946	5.186			
Unfavorable job stability			7 53	.4508	.2032
Aspirations	.4332	8.140			
Favorable job mobility			7 53	.3103	.0963
None					
Unfavorable job mobility			7 53	.1997	.0399
None					
Job satisfaction			6 87	.3762	.1415
Low status job reactions	-.2164	4.500			
Low status job reactions			2 177	.1274	.0162
None					
Aspirations			2 96	.5093	.2594
First job characteristics	-.4954	31.289			
Motivation			2 175	.0630	.0039
None					
Job-motivation interaction			1 180	.0514	.0026
None					

Table A11
Path Regression Results of the Analysis of the Core Model for the Subgroup Category: Age Between 18 and 20

Significant paths	BETA	F	DF	R	R^2
			11		
Occupational status 1975			120	.5833	.3402
Aspirations	.2697	10.622			
First job characteristics	.5014	25.031			
			11		
Wages 1975			120	.3364	.1131
Commitment to work ethic	-.2096	5.229			
			10		
Commitment to work ethic			121	.3464	.1200
First job characteristics	.2779	6.106			
			7		
Unfavorable job stability			124	.1625	.0264
None					
			7		
Favorable job mobility			124	.1301	.0169
None					
			7		
Unfavorable job mobility			124	.2098	.0440
None					
			6		
Job satisfaction			212	.3717	.1382
Motivation	.1420	4.820			
Aspirations	-.1425	4.255			
Low status job reactions	-.1699	7.003			
			2		
Low status job reactions			435	.0526	.0028
None					
			2		
Aspirations			216	.2961	.0877
First job characteristics	-.2961	20.762			
			2		
Motivation			428	.0472	.0022
None					
			1		
Job-motivation interaction			445	.0257	.0007
None					

Table A12
Path Regression Results of the Analysis of the Core Model for the Subgroup Category: Age Between 21 and 24

Significant paths	BETA	F	DF	R	R^2
Occupational status 1975			11 244	.6892	.4749
Aspirations	.2083	15.549			
First job characteristics	.6683	121.945			
Wages 1975			11 244	.4365	.1905
Commitment to work ethic	-.1455	6.113			
Aspirations	.1389	4.485			
First job characteristics	.4142	30.380			
Commitment to work ethic			10 245	.2065	.0427
Unfavorable job stability	-.1679	4.302			
Unfavorable job stability			7 248	.2974	.0884
Tenure on first job	.1893	9.602			
Favorable job mobility			7 248	.1647	.0271
None					
Unfavorable job mobility			7 248	.2865	.0821
First job characteristics	-.1921	6.047			
Tenure on first job	-.1503	6.007			
Job satisfaction			6 378	.3850	.1482
Job-motivation interaction	.1186	4.283			
Aspirations	-.2630	25.441			
Low status job reactions	-.1953	16.561			
Low status job reactions			2 655	.0514	.0027
None					
Aspirations			2 382	.3924	.1540
First job characteristics	-.3935	69.245			
Motivation			2 654	.0170	.0003
None					
Job-motivation interaction			1 658	.0006	.0000
None					

APPENDIX B

I. CATEGORICAL VARIABLES

Job Mobility-Satisfaction Index[a]

Label	Absolute frequency	Relative frequency (percent)	Adjusted frequency (percent)
Favorable job stability	143	10.2	20.8
Unfavorable job stability	187	13.4	27.1
Favorable job mobility	172	12.3	25.0
Unfavorable job mobility	187	13.4	27.1
Missing	711	50.8	---
Total	1400	100.1[b]	100.0[b]

a. Index created from two variables, job satisfaction 1971 and change in employer 1966-1971, and converted into dummy variables with the first category used as the reference group.

b. In this and the ensuing tables, frequencies may not add up perfectly to 100 percent due to rounding.

Low Status Job Reactions[a]

Label	Absolute frequency	Relative frequency (percent)	Adjusted frequency (percent)
No	947	67.6	72.0
Yes	368	26.3	28.0
Missing	85	6.1	---
Total	1400	100.0	100.0

a. Dummy variable created from following responses to question asking about first factor disliked most about current job: work is difficult, work is dangerous, work is monotonous, work involves little or no responsibility, earnings, job insecurity, work not steady, lack of seniority, supervision, no chance of advancement.

Marital Status[a]

Label	Absolute frequency (percent)	Relative frequency (percent)
Married, spouse present	563	40.2
Married, spouse absent	32	2.3
Widowed	1	0.1
Divorced	19	1.4
Separated	31	2.2
Never married	754	53.9
Total	1400	100.1

a. Variable converted into three dummy variables, incorporating the third, fourth, and fifth categories into one dummy and using the second category as the reference group.

Motivation[a]

Label	Absolute frequency (percent)	Relative frequency (percent)	Adjusted frequency (percent)
Extrinsic	610	43.6	46.9
Intrinsic	691	49.4	53.1
Missing	99	7.1	---
Total	1400	100.1	100.0

a. Variable created from grouping responses to question, asking about first factor liked most about first job, into indicated categories.

Race

Label	Absolute frequency (percent)	Relative frequency (percent)	Adjusted frequency (percent)
Black	396	28.3	28.5
White	995	71.1	71.5
Missing	9	0.6	---
Total	1400	100.0	100.0

Region of Residence[a]

Region	Absolute frequency (percent)	Relative frequency (percent)
New England	70	5.0
Middle Atlantic	242	17.3
East North Central	266	19.0
West North Central	89	6.4
South Atlantic	307	21.9
East South Central	101	7.2
West South Central	139	9.9
Mountain	47	3.4
Pacific	139	9.9
Total	1400	100.0

a. Variable converted into eight dummy variables, leaving the last category—Pacific—as the reference group.

Sex

Label	Absolute frequency (percent)	Relative frequency (percent)
Female	657	46.9
Male	743	53.1
Total	1400	100.0

Urbanization[a]

Label	Absolute frequency (percent)	Relative frequency (percent)	Adjusted frequency (percent)
SMSA central city	467	33.4	33.4
SMSA not in central city	388	27.7	27.7
Not in SMSA	544	38.9	38.9
Missing	1	0.1	---
Total	1400	100.1	100.0

a. Variable converted into two dummy variables, leaving the third category—not in SMSA—as the reference group.

II. CONTINUOUS VARIABLES

A. Variables with Substantive Categories

Age

Years	Absolute frequency (percent)	Relative frequency (percent)	Category frequency
14	4	0.3	
15	11	0.8	
16	32	2.3	141
17	94	6.7	
18	145	10.4	
19	179	12.8	523
20	199	14.2	
21	195	13.9	
22	202	14.4	736
23	191	13.6	
24	148	10.6	
Total	1400	100.0	

mean 20.576 s.d. 2.263 median 20.685

Community Size

Code	Label	Absolute frequency (percent)	Relative frequency (percent)
1	Urban > 3 million	261	18.6
2	Urban 1 - 3 million	142	10.1
3	Urban 250 - 999,000	164	11.7
4	Urban < 250,000	154	11.0
5	Urban 25,000	52	3.7
6	Urban 10 - 25,000	56	4.0
7	Urban 2.5 - 10,000	91	6.5
8	Rural	480	34.3
	Total	1400	99.9

mean 4.804 s.d. 2.798 median 4.364

Job Satisfaction

Code	Label	Absolute frequency (percent)	Relative frequency (percent)	Adjusted frequency (percent)
1	Dislike very much	40	2.9	2.9
2	Dislike somewhat	85	6.1	6.2
3	Like fairly well	508	36.3	36.8
4	Like very much	746	53.3	54.1
-999	Missing	21	1.5	---
	Total	1400	100.1	100.0

mean 3.421 s.d. 0.736 median 3.576

Tenure on First Job

Years	Absolute frequency (percent)	Relative frequency (percent)	Adjusted frequency (percent)
0	641	45.8	50.5
1	182	13.0	14.3
2	223	15.9	17.6
3	109	7.8	8.6
4	53	3.8	4.2
5	21	1.5	1.7
6	27	1.9	2.1
7	13	0.9	1.0
Missing	131	9.4	---
Total	1400	100.0	100.0

mean 1.202 s.d. 1.590 median 0.490

B. Variables with Numerical Categories

Name	Range minimum-maximum	Mean	S.D.	Median	Comments
Aspirations	-44 84	14.523	21.339	7.692	Difference score of Duncan index of occupation of job desired at age 30 (35 for women) and occupation of current 1966 job
Commitment to work ethic	45.217 127.625	100.299	15.876	103.353	Index created from unweighted summation of two 1971 internal-external locus of control variables—one specific, the other overall—both normalized and transformed to positive numbers
First job characteristics	75.349 134.178	93.889	11.517	92.218	Index created from unweighted summation of 1966 occupational status and wages variables normalized using z-scores and further transformed to positive numbers
Intelligence	44.445 149.757	102.237	15.459	104.406	Index created from unweighted summation of standardized IQ score and a standardized Knowledge of World of Work total score, both of which were transformed to positive numbers
Job-motivation interaction	0.755 2.563	1.653	0.479	1.755	Interaction variable created as unweighted multiplicative function of the first job characteristics variable, adjusting the decimal, and a job motivation variable
Schooling	45.176 149.467	98.936	14.436	96.908	Index created from unweighted summation of standardized education and training variables, both of which were transformed to positive numbers
Socioeconomic status	3 93	31.028	22.762	18.943	Duncan index of parent's occupation, using mother's occupation if and only if father's occupation was missing

B. Variables with Numerical Categories (continued)

Name	Range minimum-maximum	Mean	S.D.	Median	Comments
Occupational status 1975	0 93	38.395	22.460	38.971	Duncan index of 1975 occupational status
Unemployment rate	5 115	41.978	16.302	38.693	Unemployment rate of labor market of the 1966 residence, adjusting the decimal
Wages 1975	0 50,000	7088.24	6743.76	5999.93	Income from wages and salary in past year, assessed in 1975

REFERENCES

Aldag, R.J. and A.P. Brief. Examination of alternative models of job satisfaction. *Human Relations,* 1978, *31,* 91-98.

Almquist, E.Mc. *Minorities, gender, and work.* Lexington, MA: D.C. Heath, 1979.

Altimus, C.A. and R.J. Tersine. Chronological age and job satisfaction: The young blue collar worker. *Academy of Management Journal,* 1973, *16,* 53-66.

Anderson, T.W. *Introduction to multivariate statistical analysis.* New York: Wiley, 1958.

Andrisani, P., E. Appelbaum, R. Koppel, and R. Miljus. *Work attitudes and labor market experience: Evidence from the National Longitudinal Surveys.* A report prepared for the Employment and Training Administration of the Department of Labor, 1977.

Argyris, C. *Personality and organization.* New York: Harper, 1957.

_______ *Integrating the individual and the organization.* New York: Wiley, 1964.

_______ Personality and organization theory revisited. *Administrative Science Quarterly,* 1973, *18,* 141-167.

Bass, B.M. *Organizational psychology.* Boston: Allyn and Bacon, 1965.

Bass, B.M. and G.V. Barrett. *Man, work and organizations.* Boston: Allyn and Bacon, 1972.

Baxter, J.L. The chronic job changer: A study of youth unemployment. *Social and Economic Administration,* 1975, *9,* 184-206.

Becker, G.S. *The economics of discrimination.* Chicago: University of Chicago Press, 1957.

_______ *Human capital.* New York: Columbia University Press, 1964.

Berg, I. They won't work: The end of the protestant ethic and all that. In J. O'Toole (Ed.), *Work and the quality of life.* Cambridge, MA: The MIT Press, 1974.

Bergmann, B. The effect on white incomes of discrimination in employment. *Journal of Political Economy,* 1971, *79,* 294-313.

Berryman, S.E. Youth unemployment and career education: Reasonable expectations. *Public Policy,* 1978, *26,* 29-69.

Blalock, H.M. *Causal inferences in nonexperimental research.* Chapel Hill: University of North Carolina, 1964.

_______ Path coefficients versus regression coefficients. *American Journal of Sociology,* 1967, *72,* 675-676.

Blau, P.M. and O.D. Duncan. *The American occupational structure.* New York: Wiley, 1967.

Blauner, R. *Alienation and freedom.* Chicago: University of Chicago Press, 1964.

Blood, M.R. Work values and job satisfaction. *Journal of Applied Psychology,* 1969, *53,* 456-459.

Blood, M.R. and C.L. Hulin. Alienation, environmental characteristics and worker responses. *Journal of Applied Psychology,* 1967, *51,* 284-290.

Boudon, R. A method of linear causal analysis: Dependence analysis. *American Sociological Review,* 1965, *30,* 365-374.

Bray, E.W., R.J. Campbell, and D.L. Grant. *Formative years in business: A long-term A.T.&T. study of managerial lives.* New York: Wiley, 1974.

Brayfield, A.H. and W.H. Crockett. Employee attitudes and performance. *Psychological Bulletin,* 1955, *52,* 396-428.

Brayfield, A.H. and R.V. Wells. Interrelationships among measures of job satisfaction and general satisfaction. *Journal of Applied Psychology,* 1957, *41,* 201-205.

Brief, A.P. and R.J. Aldag. Employee reactions to job characteristics: A constructive replication. *Journal of Applied Psychology,* 1975, *60,* 182-186.

Bullock, P. *Aspirations vs. opportunity and careers in the inner city.* Institute of Labor and Industrial Relations: University of Michigan, 1973.

Burt, R.S. Confirmatory factor analytic structures and the theory construction process. *Sociological Methods and Research,* 1973, *2,* 131-190.

Cain, G.G. *Married women in the labor force.* Chicago: University of Chicago Press, 1966.

________ *The challenge of dual and radical theories of the labor market to orthodox theory.* Paper presented at the American Economics Association Annual Meetings, 1975.

Carter, M.D. *Home, school and work: A study of the education and employment of young people in Britain.* London: Pergamon Press, 1962.

________ *Into work.* Baltimore: Penguin, 1966.

Centers, R. Motivational aspects of job satisfaction. *Journal of Social Psychology,* 1948, *27,* 187-217.

Chow, G.C. Tests of equality between sets of coefficients in two linear regressions. *Econometrica,* 1960, *28,* 591-605.

Corcoran, M. and C. Jencks. Effects of family background on occupational status. Chapter 2 in C. Jencks and L. Rainwater, *The effects of family background, test scores, personality traits and education on economic success.* Springfield, VA: National Technical Information Service, 1977.

Davis, L.E. Enhancing the quality of working life developments in the United States. *International Labor Review,* 1977, *116,* 53-65.

Davis, L.E. and A.B. Cherns. *The quality of working life.* Vol. 1. New York: The Free Press, 1975.

Dewhurst, H.D. and R.D. Arvey. Range of interests vs. job performance and satisfaction. *Research Management,* 1976, *19,* 18-23.

Dodson, C. and B. Haskew. Why public workers stay. *Public Personnel Management,* 1976, *5,* 132-138.

Doeringer, P.B. and J. Dunlop. *Programs to employ the disadvantaged.* Englewood Cliffs, NJ: Prentice Hall, 1969.

Doeringer, P.B. and M. Piore. *Internal labor markets and manpower analysis.* Lexington, MA: D.C. Heath, 1971.

Doob, L.W. The behavior of attitudes. *Psychological Review,* 1947, *54,* 135-156.

Dubin, R. Industrial workers' worlds: A study of the "central life interests" of industrial workers. *Social Problems,* 1956, *3,* 131-142.

Dubin, R. and J.E. Champoux. Central life interests and job satisfaction. *Organizational Behavior and Human Performance,* 1977, *18,* 366-377.

Dubin, R., J.E. Champoux, L.W. Porter, and E. Stone. Central life interests and organizational commitment of blue collar and clerical workers. *Administrative Science Quarterly,* 1975, *20,* 411-421.

Dubin, R. and L.W. Porter. Implications of differential job perceptions. *Industrial Relations,* 1974, *27,* 265-273.

Duncan, O.D. A socioeconomic index for all occupations. In A.J. Reiss (Ed.), *Occupations and social status.* Glencoe, IL: The Free Press, 1961.

_______ Inheritance of poverty or inheritance of race? In D.P. Moynihan (Ed.), *On understanding poverty.* New York: Basic Books, 1968.

_______ *Introduction to structural equation models.* New York: Academic Press, 1975.

Duncan, O.D., D.L. Featherman, and B. Duncan. *Socioeconomic background and achievement.* New York: Seminar Press, 1972.

Dunham. R.B. Reactions to job characteristics: Moderating effects of the organization. *Academy of Management Journal,* 1977, *20,* 42-65.

Dunnette, M.D., R. Avery, and P. Banas. Why do they leave? *Personnel,* 1973, *50,* 25-39.

Falk, W.W. and A.G. Cosby. Woman and the status attainment process. *Social Science Quarterly,* 1975, *56,* 307-314.

Farris, G.F. A predictive study of turnover. *Personnel Psychology,* 1971, *24,* 311-328.

Featherman, D.L. and R.M. Hauser. Sexual inequalities and socioeconomic achievement in the U.S., 1962-1973. *American Sociological Review,* 1976, *41,* 462-483.

Festinger, L. *A theory of cognitive dissonance.* Evanston, IL: Row, Peterson, 1957.

Foulkes, F.K. *Creating more meaningful work.* New York: American Management Association, 1969.

Freestone, P.M. Vocational interests of elementary school children. *Occupational Psychology,* 1939, *13.*

Fremon, C. *The occupational patterns in urban employment change, 1965-67.* Washington: The Urban Institute, 1970.

Gannon, M.J. and D.H. Hendrickson. Career orientation and job satisfaction among working wives. *Journal of Applied Psychology,* 1973, *57,* 339-340.

Gibson, J.L. and S.M. Klein. Employee attitudes as a function of age and length of service: A reconceptualization. *Academy of Management Journal,* 1970, *13,* 411-425.

Gilroy, C.L. Job losers, leavers and entrants: Traits and trends. *Monthly Labor Review,* 1973, *96,* 13-15.

Ginzberg, E. *The manpower connection: Education and work.* Cambridge, MA: The Harvard University Press, 1975.

Goldberger, A.S. *Econometric theory.* New York: Wiley, 1964.

________ *Topics in regression analysis.* New York: Macmillan, 1968.

Goodwin, L. *Do the poor want to work?* Washington: The Brookings Institution, 1972.

Gordon, D.M. (Ed.). *Problems in political economy.* Lexington, MA: D.C. Heath, 1971.

________ (Ed.). *Theories of poverty and underemployment.* Lexington, MA: D.C. Heath, 1972.

Grasso, J.T. and J.R. Shea. *Vocational education and training: Impact on youth.* Berkeley, CA: The Carnegie Council on Policy Studies in Higher Education, 1979.

Griffin, L.J. Causal modeling of psychological success in work organizations. *Academy of Management Journal,* 1977, *20,* 6-33.

Gurin, G., J. Veroff, and S. Feld. *Americans view their mental health.* New York: Basic Books, 1960.

Hackman, J.R. and E.E. Lawler, Employee reactions to job characteristics. *Journal of Applied Psychology,* 1971, *55,* 259-286.

Hackman, J.R. and G.R. Oldham. Development of the job diagnostic survey. *Journal of Applied Psychology,* 1975, *60,* 159-170.

Hackman, J.R. and J.L. Suttle. *Improving life at work: Behavioral science approaches to organizational change.* Santa Monica, CA: Goodyear, 1977.

Hall, D.T. and E.E. Lawler. Job characteristics and pressures and the organizational integration of professionals. *Administrative Science Quarterly,* 1970, *15,* 271-281.

Hall, D.T. and R. Mansfield. Organizational and individual response to external stress. *Administrative Science Quarterly,* 1971, *16,* 533-547.

_______ Relationships of age and seniority with career variables of engineers and scientists. *Journal of Applied Psychology,* 1975, *60,* 201-210.

Hall, D.T. and K. Nougaim. An examination of Maslow's need hierarchy in an organization setting. *Organization Behavior and Human Performance,* 1968, *3,* 12-35.

Hall, D.T., B. Schneider, and H.T. Nygren. Personal factors in organizational identification. *Administrative Science Quarterly,* 1970, *15,* 176-190.

Halloran, J.D. *Attitude formation and change.* Leicester: Leicester University Press, 1967.

Hanushek, E.A. and J.E. Jackson. *Statistical methods for social scientists.* New York: Academic Press, 1977.

Hare, N. Recent trends in the occupational mobility of negroes, 1930-1960: An intra-cohort analysis. *Social Forces,* 1965, *44,* 166-173.

Harrison, B. Human capital, black poverty, and "radical" economics. *Industrial Relations,* 1971, *10,* 277-286.

_______ Education and underemployment in the urban ghetto. *The American Economic Review,* 1972, *62,* 796-811.

Hauser, R.M. and D.L. Featherman. *The process of stratification.* New York: Academic Press, 1977.

Hazer, J.T. Job satisfaction: A possible integration of two theories. *Training and Development Journal,* 1976, *30,* 12-14.

Heise, D.R. Problems in path analysis and causal inference. In E.F. Borgatta and G.W. Bohrnstedt (Eds.), *Sociological methodology.* San Francisco: Jossey-Bass, 1969.

Hennig, M. and A. Jardim. *The managerial woman.* Garden City, NY: Anchor Press/Doubleday, 1977.

Herman, J.B., R.B. Dunham, and C.L. Hulin. Organizational structure, demographic characteristics, and employee responses. *Organizational Behavior and Human Performance,* 1975, *13,* 206-232.

Herzberg, F. *Work and the nature of man.* Cleveland: World, 1966.

________ What people want from their jobs. *Industry Week,* 1970, *167,* 52-54.

Herzberg, F., B. Mausner, and B.B. Snyderman. *The motivation to work.* New York: Wiley, 1959.

Herzberg, F., B. Mausner, R.O. Peterson, and D.F. Capwell. *Job attitudes: Review of research and opinion.* Pittsburgh: Psychological Service of Pittsburgh, 1957.

Hinrichs, J. and L. Mischkind. Empirical and theoretical limitations of the two-factor hypothesis of job satisfaction. *Journal of Applied Psychology,* 1967, *51,* 191-200.

Homans, G.C. Bringing men back in. In A.H. Rubinstein and C.J. Haberstroh (Eds.), *Irwin-Dorsey series in behavioral sciences in business.* Homewood, IL: Irwin-Dorsey, 1966.

Hoppock, R. *Job satisfaction.* New York: Harper, 1935.

Hrebiniak, L.G. and M.R. Roteman. A study of the relationship between need satisfaction and absenteeism among managerial personnel. *Journal of Applied Psychology,* 1973, *58,* 381-383.

Hulin, C.L. and M.R. Blood. Job enlargement, individual differences, and worker responses. *Psychological Bulletin,* 1968, *69,* 41-65.

Hulin, C.L. and P.C. Smith. A linear model of job satisfaction. *Journal of Applied Psychology,* 1965, *49,* 209-216.

Hulin, C.L. and L.K. Waters. Regression analysis of three variations of the two-factor hypothesis of job satisfaction. *Journal of Applied Psychology,* 1971, *55,* 211-217.

Hunt, J.McV. Motivation inherent in information processing and action. In O.J. Harvey (Ed.), *Motivation and social interaction: Cognitive determinants.* New York: Ronald Press, 1963.

Hunt, J.W. and P.N. Saul. The relationship of age, tenure and job satisfaction in males and females. *Academy of Management Journal,* 1975, *18,* 690-702.

Jacobs, J.L. Satisfaction with your job a life-time concern. *Advanced Management Journal,* 1977, *42,* 44-50.

Jencks, C., M. Smith, H. Acland, M.J. Bane, D. Cohen, H. Gintis, B. Heyns, and S. Michelson. *Inequality.* New York: Basic Books, 1972.

Johnston, D.F. Future of work: Three possible alternatives. *Monthly Labor Review,* 1972, *95,* 3-11.

Johnston. J. *Econometric methods.* New York: McGraw-Hill, 1972.

Jones, A.P., L.R. James, and J.R. Bruni. Perceived leadership behavior and employee confidence in the leader as moderated by job involvement. *Journal of Applied Psychology,* 1975, *60,* 146-149.

Jones, A.P., L.R. James, J.R. Bruni, and S.B. Sells. Black-white differences in work environment perceptions and job satisfaction and its correlates. *Personnel Psychology,* 1977, *30,* 5-16.

Jones, C.F. *Economic geography.* New York: Macmillan, 1967.

Joreskog, K.G. Some contributions to maximum likelihood factor analysis. *Psychometrika,* 1967, *32,* 443-482.

Kahn, R.L. The meaning of work: Interpretation and proposals for measurement. In A.A. Campbell and P.E. Converse (Eds.), *The human meaning of social change.* New York: Russell Sage, 1972.

________ The work module: A proposal for the humanization of work. In J.O'Toole (Ed.), *Work and the quality of life.* Cambridge, MA: The MIT Press, 1974.

Kahn, R.L., D.M. Wolfe, R.D. Quinn, J.D. Snoek, and R.A. Rosenthal. *Organizational stress.* New York: Wiley, 1964.

Kaplan, H.R., C. Tausky, and R. Bolaria. Job enrichment. *Personnel Journal,* 1969, *48,* 791-798.

Kasl, S. Work and mental health. In J. O'Toole (Ed.), *Work and the quality of life.* Cambridge, MA: The MIT Press, 1974.

Katz, R. Job longevity as a situational factor in job satisfaction. *Administrative Science Quarterly,* 1978, *23,* 204-223.

Katzell, R. and D. Yankelovich. *Work productivity and job satisfaction.* New York: Harcourt, Brace, Jovanovich, 1975.

Kavanagh, M.J. and M. Halpern. The impact of job level and sex differences on the relationship between life and job satisfaction. *Academy of Management Journal,* 1977, *20,* 66-73.

Keller, T. and A.D. Szilagyi. Employee reactions to leader reward behavior. *Academy of Management Journal,* 1976, *19,* 619-625.

Kiesler, C.A., B.E. Collins, and N. Miller. *Attitude change.* New York: Wiley, 1969.

Kohen, A.I. and P. Andrisani. *Career thresholds: A longitudinal study of the educational and labor market experience of male youth.* Vol. 4. Columbus, OH: The Ohio State University Center for Human Resource Research. Washington: U.S. Department of Labor, 1973.

Kohen, A.I. J.T. Grasso, S.C. Myers, and P.M. Shields. *Career thresholds: A longitudinal study of the educational and labor market experience of young men.* Vol. 6. Columbus, OH: The Ohio State University Center for Human Resource Research. Washington: U.S. Department of Labor, 1977.

Kohen, A.I. and H.S. Parnes. *Career thresholds: A longitudinal study of the educational and labor market experience of male youth.* Vol. 3. Columbus, OH: The Ohio State University Center for Human Resource Research. Washington: U.S. Department of Labor, 1971.

Kohn, M.L. and C. Schooler. Occupational experience and psychological functioning: An assessment of reciprocal effects. *American Sociological Review,* 1973, *38,* 97-118.

Lawler, E.E. Job design and employee motivation. *Personnel Psychology,* 1969, *22,* 426-435.

________ Job attitudes and employee motivation: Theory, research and practice. *Personnel Psychology,* 1970, *23,* 223-237.

________ *Motivation in work organizations.* Monterey, CA: Brooks/Cole, 1973.

Lawler, E.E., J.R. Hackman, and S. Kaufman. Effects of job redesign: A field experiment. *Journal of Applied Social Psychology,* 1973, *3,* 49-62.

Lawler, E.E. and D.T. Hall. Relationship of job characteristics to job involvement, satisfaction, and intrinsic motivation. *Journal of Applied Psychology,* 1970, *54,* 305-312.

Lawler, E.E. and L.W. Porter. Perceptions regarding management compensation. *Industrial Relations,* 1963, *3,* 41-49.

________ The effect of performance on job satisfaction. *Industrial Relations,* 1967, *7,* 20-28.

Leiberson, S. and G.V. Fuguitt. Negro-white occupational differences in the absence of discrimination. *American Journal of Sociology,* 1967, *73,* 188-200.

Lewin, K., T. Dembo, L. Festinger, and P. Sears. Level of aspiration. In J.M. Hunt (Ed.), *Personality and the behavior disorders.* New York: Ronald Press, 1944.

Likert, R. *The human organization.* New York: McGraw-Hill, 1967.

Locke, E. What is job satisfaction. *Organizational Behavior and Human Performance,* 1969, *4,* 309-336.

Lodahl, T.M. Patterns of job attitudes in two assembly technologies. *Administrative Science Quarterly,* 1964, *8,* 482-519.

Lodahl, T.M. and M. Kejner. The definition and measurement of job involvement. *Journal of Applied Psychology,* 1965, *49,* 24-33.

MacEachron, A.E. Job level, individual differences and job satisfaction: An interaction approach. Unpublished doctoral dissertation. Cornell University, 1975.

________ Two interactive perspectives on the relationship between life and job satisfaction. *Organizational Behavior and Human Performance,* 1977, *19,* 226-246.

Macy, B.A. and D.H. Mirvis. Methodology for assessment of quality of work life and organizational effectiveness in behavioral economic terms. *Administrative Science Quarterly,* 1976, *21,* 212-222.

Maizels, J. *Adolescent needs and the transition from school to work.* University of London: The Athlone Press, 1970.

Malewski, A. Some limitations of the theory of cognitive dissonance. *Polish Psychological Bulletin,* 1964, no. 1, 7-15.

Malinvaud, E. (Trans. by A. Silvey) *Statistical methods of econometrics.* Amsterdam: North-Holland Publishing Co., 1978.

Mannheim, B. A comparative study of work centrality, job rewards and satisfaction. *Sociology of Work and Occupations,* 1975, *2,* 79-102.

Manpower Report of the President, Transmitted to the Congress, April 1974.

Marion, B.W. and S.E. Trieb. Job orientation—a factor in employee performance and turnover. *Personnel Journal,* 1969, *10,* 799-804.

Maslow, A.H. *Motivation and personality (2nd. ed.).* New York: Harper and Row, 1970.

Maurer, J.G. *Work role involvement of industrial supervisors.* East Lansing: M.S.U. Business Studies, 1969.

McCall, M. and E.E. Lawler. High school students' perception of work. *Academy of Management Journal,* 1976, *19,* 17-24.

McClendon, Mc.J. The occupational status attainment processes of males and females. *American Sociological Review,* 1976, *41,* 52-64.

McGregor, D. *The human side of enterprise.* New York: McGraw-Hill, 1960.

Merryman, C. and E. Shani. Growth and satisfaction of employees in organizations. *Personnel Journal,* 1976, *55,* 492-494.

Miller, N. Career choice, job satisfaction and the truth behind the Peter Principle. *Personnel,* 1976, *53,* 58-65.

Mitchell, T.R. and A. Biglan. Instrumentality theories: Current uses in psychology. *Psychological Bulletin,* 1971, *76,* 432-454.

Morse, N. *Satisfaction in the white collar job.* Ann Arbor, MI: University of Michigan Press, 1953.

Near, J.P., R.W. Rice, and R.G. Hunt. Work and extra-work correlates of life and job satisfaction. *Academy of Management Journal,* 1978, *21,* 248-264.

Netzer, D. *Economics and urban problems.* New York: Basic Books, 1970.

Newman, J.E. Understanding the organizational structure-job attitude relationship through perceptions of the work environment. *Organizational Behavior and Human Performance,* 1975, *14,* 371-397.

Nicolaou, L.H. *Factors influencing job satisfaction in a woman's office.* Boston:Boston College, 1972.

Nie, N.H., C.H. Hull, J.G. Jenkins, K. Steinbrenner, and D.H. Bent. *Statistical package for the social sciences.* New York: McGraw-Hill, 1975.

Nunnally, J.C. *Psychometric theory.* New York: McGraw-Hill, 1967.

Oldham, G.R. Job characteristics and internal motivation: The moderating effect of interpersonal and individual variables. *Human Relations,* 1976, *29,* 559-569.

Oldham, G.R., J.R. Hackman, and J.L. Pearce. Conditions under which employees respond positively to enriched work. *Journal of Applied Psychology,* 1976, *61,* 395-403.

Olneck, M. Effects of education. Chapter 6 in C. Jencks and L. Rainwater, *The effects of family background, test scores, personality traits, and education on economic success.* Springfield, VA: National Technical Information Service, 1977.

O'Reilly, C.A., III. Personality-job fit: Implications for individual attitudes and performance. *Organizational Behavior and Human Performance,* 1977, *18,* 36-46.

O'Reilly, C.A., III and K. Roberts. Individual differences in personality, position in the organization and job satisfaction. *Organizational Behavior and Human Performance,* 1975, *14,* 144-150.

Ornstein, M.D. *Entry into the American labor force.* New York: Academic Press, 1976.

Osgood, L.E. and P.H. Tannenbaum. The principle of congruity in prediction and attitude change. *Psychological Review,* 1955, *62,* 42-55.

Parnes, H.S. *Research on labor mobility.* New York: Social Science Research Council, 1954.

________ The National Longitudinal Surveys: New vistas for labor market research. *American Economic Review,* 1975, *65,* 244-249.

Parnes, H.S. and A.I. Kohen. Occupational information and labor market status: The case of young men. *Journal of Human Resources,* 1975, *10,* 44-55.

Parnes, H.S., R.C. Miljus, R.S. Spitz, and Associates. *Career thresholds: a longitudinal study of the educational and labor market experience of male youth.* Vol. 1. Columbus, OH: The Ohio State University Center for Human Resource Research. Washington: U.S. Department of Labor, 1970.

Parnes, H.S. and R.S. Spitz. A conceptual framework for studying labor mobility. *Monthly Labor Review,* 1969, *92,* 55-58.

Patchen, M. Some questionnaire measures of employee motivation and morale. *Institute for Social Research Monograph,* 1965, *41,* 1-70.

________ *Participation, achievement and involvement on the job.* Englewood Cliffs, NJ: Prentice-Hall, 1970.

Piker, J. *Entry into the labor force: A survey of literature on the experiences of negro and white youths.* Ann Arbor, MI: Institute of Labor and Industrial Relations, 1968.

Porter, J.N. Race, socialization and mobility in educational and early occupational attainment. *American Sociological Review,* 1974, *39,* 303-316.

Porter, L.W. A study of perceived need satisfaction in bottom and middle management jobs. *Journal of Applied Psychology,* 1961, *45,* 1-10.

________ Job attitudes in management: I. perceived deficiencies in need fulfillment as a function of job level. *Journal of Applied Psychology,* 1962, *46,* 375-384.

________ Job attitudes in management: II. perceived importance of needs as a function of job level. *Journal of Applied Psychology,* 1963, *47,* 141-148.

Porter, L.W. and E.E. Lawler. Properties of organization structure in relation to job attitudes and job behavior. *Psychological Bulletin,* 1965, *64,* 25-51.

Porter, L.W. and R. Steers. Organizational, work and personal factors in employee turnover and absenteeism. *Psychological Bulletin,* 1973, *80,* 151-176.

Prybil, L.D. Job satisfaction in relation to job performance and occupational level. *Personnel Journal,* 1973, *52,* 94-100.

Quinn, J.F. Microeconomic determinants of early retirement: A cross-sectional view of white married men. *Journal of Human Resources,* 1977, *12,* 328-346.

Rabinowitz, S. An examination of the influence of individual difference variables and perceived job stimulation on job involvement. Unpublished master's thesis. Michigan State University, 1975.

Rabinowitz, S. and D.T. Hall. Organizational research on job involvement. *Psychological Bulletin,* 1977, *84,* 265-288.

Reitz, H.J. and L.N. Jewell. Sex, locus of control, and job involvement: A six county investigation. *Academy of Management Journal,* 1979, *22,* 72-80.

Reynolds, L.G. *Research on wages.* New York: Social Science Research Council, 1948.

Roos, L. Institutional change, career mobility, and job satisfaction. *Administrative Science Quarterly,* 1978, *23,* 318-333.

Rosen, R.A. World of work through the eyes of the hard core. *Personnel Administration,* 1970, *33,* 8-21.

Rosow, J.M. Job satisfaction and the blue collar blues. *Personnel,* 1971, *48,* 8-16.

Rottenberg, S. On choice in labor markets. *Industrial and Labor Relations Review,* 1956, *9,* 183-199.

Rotter, J.B. Generalized expectancies for internal versus external control of reinforcement. *Psychological Monographs,* 1966, *80,* (1, Whole No. 609).

Rousseau, D.M. Technological differences in job characteristics, employee satisfaction and motivation. *Organizational Behavior and Human Performance,* 1977, *19,* 18-42.

Runyon, K.E. Some interactions between personality variables and management styles. *Journal of Applied Psychology,* 1973, *57,* 288-294.

Salancik, G.R. and J. Pfeffer. An examination of need-satisfaction models of job attitudes. *Administrative Science Quarterly,* 1977, *22,* 427-456.

________ A social information processing approach to job attitudes and task design. *Administrative Science Quarterly,* 1978, *23,* 224-253.

Saleh, S. and J. Hosek. Job involvement: Concepts and measurements. *Academy of Management Journal,* 1976, *19,* 213-223.

Samuelson, P.S. *Economics. 9th Edition.* New York: McGraw-Hill, 1972.

Sarnoff, J. Psychoanalytic theory and social attitudes. *Public Opinion Quarterly,* 1960, *24,* 251-279.

Schein, E.H. The individual, the organization, and the career: A conceptual scheme. *Journal of Applied Behavioral Science,* 1971, *7,* 402-425.

Schmitt, N., B. Coyle, J. White, and J. Rauscherberger. Background, needs, job perceptions, and job satisfaction: A causal model. *Personnel Psychology,* 1978, *31,* 889-901.

Schneider, B., D.T. Hall, and H.T. Nygren. Self-image and job characteristics as correlates of changing organizational identification. *Human Relations,* 1971, *24,* 397-416.

Schoenberg, R. Strategies for meaningful comparison. In H.L. Costner (Ed.), *Sociological methodology.* San Francisco: Jossey-Bass, 1972.

Schwab, D.P. and L.L. Cummings. Theories of performance and satisfaction: A review. *Industrial Relations,* 1970, *9,* 408-430.

Schwyhart, W.R. and P.C. Smith. Factors in the job involvement of middle managers. *Journal of Applied Psychology,* 1972, *56,* 227-233.

Sewell, W.H., A.O. Haller, and G.W. Ohlendorf. The educational and early occupational status attainment process: Replications and revision. *American Sociological Review,* 1970, *35,* 1014-1027.

Sewell, W.H. and R.M. Hauser. *Education, occupation, and earnings.* New York: Academic Press, 1975.

Sheppard, H. Discontented blue collar workers. *Monthly Labor Review,* 1971, *94,* 25-32.

Sheppard, H. and N. Herrick. *Where have all the robots gone?* New York: Collier-Macmillan, 1972.

Siegel, A.L. Antecedents and consequences of job involvement. Unpublished master's thesis. Michigan State University, 1971.

Siegel, A.L. and R.A. Ruh. Job involvement, participation in decision making, personal background and job behavior. *Organizational Behavior and Human Performance,* 1973, *9,* 318-327.

Simon, H. *Models of man.* New York: Wiley, 1957.

Simpson, R.L. and I. Harper. Social origins, occupational advice, occupational values and work careers. *Social Forces,* 1962, *40,* 264-271.

Sommers, D. and A. Eck. Occupational mobility in the American labor force. *Monthly Labor Review,* 1977, *100,* 4-19.

Sorkin, A.I. On the occupational status of women, 1870-1970. *American Journal of Economics and Sociology,* 1973, *32,* 235-243.

Steers, R.M. Factors affecting job attitudes in a goal-setting environment. *Academy of Management Journal,* 1976, *19,* 6-16.

Strauss, G. Worker dissatisfaction: A look at the causes. *Monthly Labor Review,* 1974, *97,* 57-58.

Sullivan, J.L. Multiple indicators and complex causal models. In H.M. Blalock (Ed.), *Causal models in the social sciences.* Chicago: Aldine, 1971.

Susman, G.I. Job enlargement: Effects of culture on worker responses. *Industrial Relations,* 1973, *12,* 1-15.

Tannenbaum, A.S. *Social psychology of the work organization.* Belmont, CA: Brooks/Cole, 1966.

Thurow, L.C. *Poverty and discrimination.* Washington: The Brookings Institution, 1969.

Tiffany, D.W., J.R. Cowan, and D.M. Tiffany. *The unemployed: A social-psychological portrait.* Englewood Cliffs, NJ: Prentice-Hall, 1974.

Treas, J. Differential achievement: Race, sex, and jobs. Paper presented at the American Sociological Association Annual Meetings, New York, 1976.

Treiman, D.J. and E.K. Terrell. Sex and the process of status attainment: A comparison of working women and men. *American Sociological Review,* 1975, *40,* 174-201.

Tsuchigane, R. and N. Dodge. *Economic discrimination against women in the United States.* Lexington, MA: D.C. Heath, 1974.

Turner, A.N. and P.R. Lawrence. *Industrial jobs and the worker.* Cambridge, MA: Division of Research, Graduate School of Business, Harvard University, 1965.

Tyree, A. and J. Treas. The occupational and marital mobility of women. *American Sociological Review,* 1974, *39,* 293-302.

Umstot, D.D., C.H. Bell, Jr., and T.R. Mitchell. Effects of job enrichment and task goals on satisfaction and productivity: Implications for job design. *Journal of Applied Psychology,* 1976, *61,* 379-394.

Van der Geer, J. *Introduction to multivariate analysis for the social sciences.* San Francisco: Freeman, 1971.

Van Maanen, J. and R. Katz. Individuals and their careers: Some temporal considerations for work satisfaction. *Personnel Psychology,* 1976, *29,* 601-606.

Vardi, Y. and T. Hammer. Interorganizational mobility and career perceptions of rank and file employees in different technologies. *Academy of Management Journal,* 1977, *20,* 622-634.

Vroom, V.H. Ego-involvement, job satisfaction, and job performance. *Personnel Psychology,* 1962, *15,* 159-177.

________ *Work and motivation.* New York: Wiley, 1964.

________ *Motivation in management.* New York: American Foundation for Management Research, 1965.

Walton, R.E. Quality of working life: What is it? *Sloan Management Review,* 1973, *15,* 11-21.

Wanous, J.P. Individual differences and reactions of job characteristics. *Journal of Applied Psychology,* 1974, *59,* 616-622.

Waters, L.K., D. Roach, and N. Batlis. Organizational climate dimensions and job-related attitudes. *Personnel Psychology,* 1974, *27,* 465-476.

Weaver, C.H. Correlates of job satisfaction: Some evidence from the National Surveys. *Academy of Management Journal,* 1974, *17,* 373-375.

________ Sex differences in job satisfaction. *Business Horizons,* 1974, *17,* 43-49.

________ What workers want from their jobs. *Personnel,* 1976, *53,* 48-54.

________ Relationships among pay, race, sex, occupational prestige, supervision, work autonomy, and job satisfaction in a national sample. *Personnel Psychology,* 1977, *30,* 437-445.

Weissenberg, P. and L.W. Gruenfeld. Relationship between job satisfaction and job involvement. *Journal of Applied Psychology,* 1968, *52,* 469-473.

Westcott, D.N. Youth in the labor force: An area study. *Monthly Labor Review,* 1976, *99,* 3-9.

White, B.L. Criterion for job satisfaction: Is interesting work most important. *Monthly Labor Review,* 1977, *100,* 30-35.

White, J.K. Individual differences and the job quality—worker response relationship: Review, integration, and comments. *Academy of Management Review,* 1979, *3,* 267-280.

White, J.K. and R.A. Ruh. Effects of personal values on the relationship between participation and job attitudes. *Administrative Science Quarterly,* 1973, *18,* 506-514.

Wickert, F.R. Turnover, and employees' feelings of ego-involvement in the day-to-day operations of a company. *Personnel Psychology,* 1951, *4,* 185-197.

Winer, B.J. *Statistical principles in experimental design.* New York: McGraw-Hill, 1971.

Wnuk-Lipinski, E. Job satisfaction and the quality of working life: The Polish experience. *International Labor Review,* 1977, *115,* 53-64.

Wolfbein, S. *Education and training for full employment.* New York: Columbia University Press, 1967.

Wood, D.A. Effect of worker orientation differences on job attitude correlates. *Journal of Applied Psychology,* 1974, *59,* 54-60.

Wool, H. Future labor supply for lower level occupations. *Monthly Labor Review,* 1976, *99,* 22-31.

_______ *The labor supply for lower level occupations.* New York: Praeger Publishers, 1976.

Work in America. Report of a special task force to the Secretary of Health, Education and Welfare. Cambridge, MA: The MIT Press, 1973.

Yankelovich, D. *The changing values on campus: Political and personal attitudes on campus.* New York: Washington Square Press, 1972.

_______ Who gets ahead in America. *Psychology Today,* 1979, *13,* 28+.

Zeller, F.A., J.R. Shea, A.I. Kohen, and J.A. Meyer. *Career thresholds: A longitudinal study of the educational and labor market experience of male youth.* Vol. 2. Columbus, OH: The Ohio State University Center for Human Resource Research. Washington: U.S. Department of Labor, 1970.